Suzhou Gardens

Chen Congzhou

陈从周

（纪念版）
Commemorative Edition

苏州园林

同济大学出版社　上海

TONGJI UNIVERSITY PRESS　SHANGHAI

陈从周先生百年诞辰纪念

Commemorating the Centenary of Chen Congzhou's Birth

2018 年，因中国著名古典园林与建筑艺术家陈从周先生的百年诞辰而非同寻常。

为了这份特别的纪念，我们将陈从周先生的四部经典学术著作《苏州园林》《苏州旧住宅》《扬州园林（与住宅）》《中国名园》汇集再版。文字的重新录入与勘校，照片、测绘图的重新查找与制作……我们倾注满腔心血，将崇敬之情融入每段文字、每张图片的编排与设计之中。

为了明晰文字内容与图片之间的逻辑关系，我们在忠于原书稿素材的基础上，重新调整了图文次序，并对四本书中的照片和测绘图较原版做了局部删减。另外，因新寻找到陈从周先生当年拍摄的扬州园林照片，《扬州园林与住宅》（原《扬州园林》）较原版做了约 50 张图片的增补。

由于汇集再版的四部著作的原版来自不同的年代、不同的英文译者、不同的出版社，因此译文风格与专有名词译法迥异。加之目前园林等专有名词尚未有统一的官方译法（政府部门、景点官网、国际组织、民间等各方的译法不一），作为"纪念版"，为了尽量保持原版的历史风貌与体系完整，对于专有名词的英译，我们只做了所属书内的统一。

四部久负盛名的经典著作，再现一位建筑前辈的魁奇风骨。

——编者按

2018 is a very special year because of the centenary of a great man in the field of Chinese architecture.

To memorize the extraordinary significance, we are going to republish Mr. Chen's four classic academic works: *Suzhou Gardens*, *Traditional Suzhou Residences*, *Yangzhou Gardens (and Traditional Residences)*, and *Famous Chinese Gardens*. We have put great effort into these books, typing and proofreading texts, collecting photos and drawings, editing images... We designed and arranged the layout and pictures with the highest respect for the author.

While trying our best to maintain the authenticity of the contents, we have adjusted the sequence of the contents and deleted some photos and drawings compared to the original, so as to better clarify the relationship between texts and pictures. In addition, due to the newly discovered photos of Yangzhou gardens taken by the author, about 50 pictures in *Yangzhou Gardens and Traditional Residences* (originally *Yangzhou Gardens*) were added.

Since the original editions of the four reprinted works are from different time, translated by different translators into English, and published by different publishers, the translation styles are not alike, and the proper nouns are translated in different ways. Currently, there is no unified official translation for the proper nouns. For example, for gardens, government departments, official websites of the scene spots, international organizations, and the general public have their own English translations. As the four books published this time are "Centenary Edition", the original historical features and complete system of which should be maintained as much as possible, we have only made the translations of proper nouns consistent within each book.

The four classic works on classical Chinese gardens and residences are revived, reflecting the distinguished character of a trailblazing Chinese architectural master.

— The Editors

目录 | Table of Contents

代序 | In Lieu of Preface

我的第一本书——《苏州园林》
My First Book—*Suzhou Gardens*

To be honest, my first book should have been my earliest book. However I am a person with a wide range of interest. My earliest books are not on the line of my profession, for example, the *Biography of Poet Xu Zhimo* (《徐志摩年谱》). Besides, I wrote miscellaneous monographs on architecture. They are based on some materials I collected occasionally. The first book I wrote in real earnest should be the *Suzhou Gardens*. It was completed in1956. This is the first book on a systematic study and discussion of Suzhou gardens after 1949 when the People's Republic of China was established.

In early 1950s, I was a teacher in the Architecture Department of Tongji University in Shanghai. At the same time I did some spare-time teaching at Sunan Industrial College in Suzhou (苏州苏南工专). These classes were scheduled on Saturday morning. I took the night train on Fridays, stayed in a hotel near Guanqian Jie (观前街). Earlier next morning I went to the college located in the Garden of Canglang Ting (the Canglang Pavilion, 沧浪亭) to teach my class. After taking a siesta, I rambled in the gardens, with notebook, camera, tape measure and scratch paper at hand. "I watch leisurely mosses and berries, as my migrant interest dictates." I enjoyed the sceneries and recorded their beauty at will. On early Sunday morning, I entered the gardens again. At noon, with a pot of fragrant tea and a dish of pastries, I sat by the rockeries to savor my snack. At that time, there were few viewers in these gardens. I could linger around as long as I wish. Excited by the scenes, I was not aware of the drowsiness. It was not until sunset that I left gardens with full satisfaction, and took the train back to Shanghai. My kids were waiting for me at the door and were elated with the

我的第一本书，本应指我最早写作的；然而，像我这种兴趣多方面的人，最初写的书并不是我的本行，例如《徐志摩年谱》，还有一些零星资料收集性的建筑书籍。如果论正式写书的话，那应该算《苏州园林》了。这本书是一九五六年完成的，也是新中国成立后研究、讨论苏州园林所出版的第一部书。

二十世纪五十年代初，我在同济大学建筑系任教，同时又在苏州苏南工专（苏南工业专科学校）兼课。因为苏州的课是在星期六的上午，我星期五晚车去苏州，住在观前街附近旅馆中，第二天清晨去位于沧浪亭的该校上课。午梦初回，我信步园林，以笔记本、照相机、尺纸自随，真可说是"兴移无洒扫，随意望莓苔"。自游，自品，俯拾得之。次日煦阳初照，叩门入园，直至午阴嘉树清园，香茗佐点，小酌山间。那时游人稀少，任我盘桓，忘午倦之侵人也。待到夕阳红半，尽一日之兴，我也上火车站，载兴而归。儿辈倚门相待，以苏州茶食迎得一笑，如今，他们的年龄正与我当年相仿佛。《苏州园林》前年在日本再版了，都已经是第二代了。

我这样每周乐此不疲，经过几年的资料累积与所见所想，开始写我的文章。我的这些立论并不是凭空而来，是实中求虚，自信尚有所据者。情以游兴，本来中国园林就是"文人园"，它是以诗情画意作主导思想的；因此，在图片中，很自然地流露出过去所说的前人词句。我于是在每张图片下，撷了宋词题上。我将一本造园的科技书以文学化出之，似乎是感到清新的。书出版后，受到了读者的赞誉与好评，但一九五八年却因此受到了批判，说我"士大夫的意识浓厚"，我只好低头认罪，承认思想没有改造好。可是事隔近卅年，在文理相通的新提法下，创造诗情画意的造园事业中，我当年的"谬举"又为人所颂了。"含泪中的微笑"，在我第一本书中，有着这样不平凡的经历啊！

从这第一本书后，虽然留下过一点"疮痕"，但我并没有气馁，我仍坚持着我的写作，到如今更有了新的发展。在这里我体会到，对一个为学

Suzhou delicacies I brought back. Now they are as old as I was at that time. It is already the era of my next generation when the second edition of my book *Suzhou Gardens* came to light in Japan the year before last.

I did the same every week for the next few years. I derived great pleasure from the excursions. Then I started to write the book based on the material and the thoughts I accumulated during this period. My viewpoints presented in the book are abstracted from the factual materials I have collected, and so, I believe, are fully substantiated. Touring the gardens triggered noble sentiment. Chinese gardens in essence catered to artists and men of letters. Therefore, the design and construction are underlined by poetic grace and picturesque romance. So naturally when I sorted out and edited the photographs I had taken of the gardens, I recalled those sentences and phrases from our ancients' poems. I entitled each photo with words or phrases from Songci. As a result, I unwittingly turned a professional book on garden architecture into a literary writing. This seemed an act of originality on my part. After it was published, the book was highly acclaimed by the readers. But later in 1958, to my surprise, I became a target of criticism for the so called feudalistic scholar's ideas in the book. I had no way out but to bow to these accusations against the alleged outworn concept of mine. Almost 30 years later, with the new-emerging advocacy of closer integraion of science with humanities, garden construction began to be imbued with artistic imagination and poetic inspiration. My much depreciated "absurdities" of the past was again highly appreciated by the public. "Smiling with tears" is what my first book offers me.

My first book left me with a bit of "trauma", but I have not been disheartened. In these years I have never relaxed my efforts to write and up till now made much headway. To a learner, perseverance is the most important motive force in life. There is no easy path in one's career. Sink or swim, all depends on whether one has courage to pursue the objective one has correctly chosen. I have a very peculiar aftertaste each time I pick up my first book. "Three decades of joy and woe all arise from Suzhou; on recalling it I'm still tender-hearted and full of yearning." My passion for Suzhou and its gardens is still smouldering, to tell you the truth.

I am gaining on age now. However, "The Heaven pities the somber grass; the Earth cherishes the golden twilight." I expect to spend the remainder of my life writing more books in dedication to my beloved people and country.

Chen Congzhou

Originally published in
News of Books (《书讯报》), Jan. 5th, 1985

的人来说，毅力是最大的动力；世界上没有平坦的道路，方向正确后，在于你有没有勇气走。如今，我每见到这本《苏州园林》，总是别有一番滋味——"我有柔情忘未了，卅年恩怨尽苏州"。我想这样来讲，我的感情还是真实的。

近三十年的年华过去了，我也垂垂老矣。然而"天意怜幽草，人间爱晚晴"，我还应该继续发挥余热，能为社会主义祖国文化事业再写几本书，我这样期望着。

陈从周

原载于一九八五年一月五日《书讯报》

苏州园林初步分析
Analysis of Suzhou Gardens

一

我国园林，如从历史上溯源的话，当推古代的"囿"与"园"，以及《汉制考》上所称的"苑"。《周礼·天官·大宰》："九职二曰园圃，毓草木。"《地官·囿人》："掌囿游之兽禁。牧百兽。"《地官·载师》："以场圃任园地。"《说文》："囿，苑有垣也。一曰禽兽曰囿。圃，种菜曰圃。园，所以树果也。苑，所以养禽兽也。"据此则囿、园、苑的含义已明。我们知道豨韦的囿、黄帝的圃已开囿圃之端，到了三代（夏、商、周），苑囿专为狩猎的地方，例如周姬昌（文王）的囿，刍荛雉兔，与民同利。秦汉以后，园林渐渐变为统治者游乐的地方，兴建楼馆，藻饰华丽了。秦嬴政（始皇）筑秦宫，跨渭水南北，覆压三百余里。汉刘彻（武帝）营上林苑、甘泉苑以及建章宫北的太液池，在历史的记载上都是范围很大的。其后，刘武（梁孝王）的兔园开了叠山的先河。魏曹丕（文帝）更有芳林园。隋杨广（炀帝）造西苑。唐李漼（懿宗）于苑中造山植木，建为园林。北宋赵佶（徽宗）

PART ONE

The origin of Chinese gardens may be traced to You (囿) and Yuan (园) of ancient China, or Yuan (苑) in the book *A Study of the Han Dynasty Customs* (《汉制考》). All these Chinese characters mean "fenced land". According to the first Chinese etymological dictionary *Explanation of Characters* (《说文》, written in 2nd century AD) You (囿) and Yuan (苑) are designed for the purpose of keeping and breeding animals, while Yuan (园) and Pu (圃) are created as a means of growing fruits and vegetables respectively. People are assigned in charge of these lands. According to *Rites of Zhou* (《周礼》, written in the Warring States period), the primary Administrator (大宰) of the Heaven Office (天官) ordained nine duties to the commoners, the second of which is to manage Yuan (园) or Pu (圃) by way of cultivating trees and grass. Also recorded in *Rites of Zhou* is that the Manager of You (囿人) in the Earth Office (地官) takes charge of shepherding and breeding animals, whereas the Master of Load (载师) cares for transforming the land into Yuan (园) and Pu (圃).

Construction of You (囿) or Pu (圃) started as early as the time of Xiwei (豨韦) or Huang Di (黄帝) respectively. Later, during the period of the three ancient Chinese dynasties—Hsia, Shang and Zhou (22nd century to 17th century BC), Yuan (苑) and You (囿) were designed as hunting grounds. For example, King Wen of the Zhou dynasty, Ji Chang (周文王，姬昌), built a You (囿) for the people to collect firewood and hunt for wild birds and rabbits.

Starting from the Qin and the Han dynasties, the function of gardens was gradually shifted into place for exclusive enjoyment of the emperor, with elaborately designed and decorated buildings. Some of them were very large according to historic records. The first emperor of a unified China, Ying Zheng of the Qin dynasty (秦始皇﹑嬴政) constructed the Palace Qin across both banks of the Wei River, covering an area of 300 Li (a distance unit used in ancient China, one Li is equal to 0.5 kilometer). Emperor Wu of the Han dynasty, Liu Che (汉武帝﹑刘彻) built Shanglin Yuan (上 林 苑), Ganquan Yuan (甘 泉 苑), as well as Taiyechi (太 液 池), to north of the Jianzhang Palace (建章宫).

Prince Xiao of Liang, Liu Wu (梁孝王﹑刘武) started to put up rockery in his Tuyuan (兔园). Emperor Wen of Wei in the Three Kindoms period, Cao Pi (魏文帝﹑曹丕) built Fanglin Yuan (芳林园) and Emperor Yang of the Sui dynasty, Yang Guang (隋炀帝﹑杨广) constructed Xiyuan (西苑). Emperor Yizong of the Tang dynasty, Li Cui (唐懿宗﹑李漼) set out to transform Yuan (苑) into a prototype of Chinese gardens by planting arbors and piling rockery in it. The garden Genyue (艮岳) built by Emperor Huizong of the Northern Song dynasty, Zhao Ji (宋徽宗﹑赵佶), is the most documented garden in historical texts.

After the Song dynasty migrated south, there were built various gardens such as Yujin (玉津), Jujing (聚景), Jifang (集芳), in the area of Lin'an (临 安 , now Hangzhou 杭 州). The emperor Kublai Khan of the Yuan dynasty (元世祖﹑忽必烈) built Taiyechi (太液池) of Long Live Hill based on the island Qionghua (琼 华 岛) of the Liao and the Jin dynasties. During the Ming and the Qing dynasties, in light of traditional customs, many new style gardens were brought into being for the sake of emperors, such as West Yuan (西 苑). South Yuan (南 苑), as well as

所营之艮岳为中国园林之最著于史籍者。宋室南渡，于临安（杭州）建造玉津、聚景、集芳等园。元忽必烈（世祖）因辽金琼华岛为万岁山太液池。明清以降，除踵前遗规外，并营建西苑、南苑，以及西郊畅春、清漪、圆明等诸园，其数目视前代更多了。

以下简述我国私家园林的发展。汉代袁广汉于洛阳北邙山下筑园，东西四里，南北五里，构石为山，复畜禽兽其间，可见其规模之大了；梁冀多规苑囿，西至弘农，东至荥阳，南入鲁阳，北到河淇，周回千里；又司农张伦造景阳山，其园林布置有若自然。可见，当时园林在建筑艺术上已有很高的造诣。尚有茹皓，吴人，采北邙及南山佳石，复筑楼馆列于上下，并引泉莳花，这些都是以人工来代天巧。六朝时期，是中国思想上起一个大转变的时代，亦是中国历史上战争最频繁的时代。士大夫习于服食，崇尚清谈，再兼以佛学昌盛，于是礼佛养性，遂萌出世之念，虽居城市，辄作山林之想。在文学方面有咏大自然的诗文；在绘画方面有山水画的出现；在建筑方面就是在第宅之旁筑园了。

石崇在洛阳建金谷园，从其《思归引序》来看，其设计主导思想是"避嚣烦"，"寄情赏"。再从《梁书·萧统传》、徐勉《戒子崧书》、庾信《小园赋》等来看，他们的言论亦不外此意。唐代，如宋之问的蓝田别墅、李德裕的平泉别墅、王维的辋川别业，皆有竹洲花坞之胜、清流翠筱之趣，人工景物，仿佛天成。而白居易的草堂尤能利用自然，参合借景的方法。宋代李格非《洛阳名园记》与周密《吴兴园林记》，前者记北宋时所存隋唐以来洛阳名园，如富郑公园等；后者记南宋吴兴园林，如沈尚书园等。记中所述，几与今日所见园林无甚二致。明清以后，园林数目远迈前代，如北京勺园、漫园，扬州影园、九峰园、马氏玲珑馆，海宁安澜园，杭州小有天园等，以及明王世贞《游金陵诸园记》所记东园等诸园，其数已不胜枚举。今日存者如杭州皋园，南浔适园、宜园、小莲庄，上海豫园，常熟燕园，南翔古漪园，无锡寄畅园等，为数尚多，而苏州一隅又为各地之冠。

下面再来看看苏州园林在历史上的发展。

Changchun (畅春), Qingyi (清漪), and Yuanmin (the Old Summer Palace, 圆明) in the western suburbs of Beijing.

The development of private gardens can be traced back to Yuan Guanghan (袁广汉) of the Han dynasty, who constructed a garden at the foot of Mount Beimang (北邙山) located north of Luoyang. This garden covered an area of four Li in the east-west direction, and five Li along the north-south direction. It was a huge garden with ranges of rockeries and a variety of animals kept within their bounds. Liang Ji (梁冀) built several Yuans and Yous which were distributed in an area thousands of Li in extension, bordered by Hongnong (弘农) to the west, Xingyang (荥阳) to the east, Luyang (鲁阳) to the south, and Heqi (河淇) to the north. Treasury Minister of the Han dynasty, Zhang Lun (汉司农，张伦), built the garden Jingyangshan (景阳山), in close imitation of natural landscape, highlighting the achievements of the art of garden architecture. In addition, Ru Hao (茹皓), an artisan of Wu region, built towers and pavilions around the grotesque rocks collected from Beimang (北邙) and Nanshan (南山), and channeled natural springs to water the garden flowers. The above-mentioned gardens were all initial attempts at imitating the sceneries of nature.

During the period of the Six Dynasties, China was undergoing a dramatic change in ideology and was inflicted with the most incessant warfare in Chinese history. A class of scholar-officials, who maintained an elegant living style, enjoyed a simple and refined life and upheld Buddhism prevalent at the time, started to think of quitting politics and to spend time worshiping Buddha for self cultivation. They hankered after an idyllic life in nature while actually residing within cities. This philosophy led to a boom in poetry eulogizing nature and an emergence of paintings depicting wild mountains and rivers. Consequently, these officials started to set up gardens adjacent to their residences in order to pursue their ideal.

The preface to the poem *Back to Nature* (《思归引序》) by Shi Chong (石崇) reveals a couple of guiding principles in the design of his Jingu Yuan (Garden of Golden Valley, 金谷园), i.e. to "avoid the hustle and bustle" and "exult in the beauty of nature". These thoughts also found their way into many other essays such as *Biography of Xiaotong* in the *Book of Liang* (《梁 书 • 萧 统 传》), *A Warning Note to My Son* by Xu Mian (徐 勉《戒子崧书》), and *Rhapsody of Garden* by Yu Xin (庚信《小园赋》) during the Northern and Southern dynasties. The gardens built during the Tang dynasty, such as Lantian Villa (蓝田别墅) of Song Zhiwen (宋 之 问), Pingquan Villa (平 泉 别 墅) of Li Deyu (李德裕), and Wangchuan Villa (辋川别业) of Wang Wei (王维), all pride in a magnificent view of bamboo islets and flowery docks and display an interest in verdant creeks and clear water. In these gardens, the man-made scenes resemble strongly those wrought by the forces of nature. On the other hand, in his Caotang (草堂), the poet Bai Juyi (白居易) incorporated elements of nature into the design by borrowing scenery from the surrounding. The article *Famous Gardens of Luoyang* (《洛阳名园记》) written by Li Gefei (李格非) of the Song dynasty records major gardens in Luoyang region from the Sui and the Tang dynasties to the Northern Song dynasty, such as the Garden of Duke Fuzheng (富郑公园). Another article of the same period by Zhou Mi (周 密), entitled *Records of Gardens in Wuxing Area* (《吴兴园林记》) documents the gardens in the Southern Song dynasty in Wuxing area, such as the Garden of Minister Shen (沈尚书园). The garden design as chronicled in these articles is already very close to that of the present day.

There was an explosive growth of gardens during the Ming and the Qing dynasties. These gardens are too numerous to be cited individually, but it is worthwhile to mention a few here just as examples, such as Shaoyuan (勺 园) and Manyuan (漫园) in Beijing; Yingyuan (影园), Jiufeng Yuan (九峰园) and Mashilinglong Guan (马 氏 玲 珑 馆) in Yangzhou; Anlan Yuan (安 澜 园) in Haining; Xiaoyoutian Yuan (小 有 天 园) in Hangzhou; as well as Dongyuan (东园) and others described in the essay *Tour of Various Gardens in Jinling* (游金陵诸园记) written by Wang Shizhen (王世贞) of the Ming dynasty.

Quite a few ancient gardens have survived up till now, such as Gaoyuan (皋园) in Hangzhou, Shiyuan (适园), Yiyuan (宜园), Xiaolianzhuang (小 莲 庄) in Nanxun, Yuyuan (豫 园) in Shanghai, Yanyuan (燕 园) in Changshu, Guyi Yuan (古漪园) in Nanxiang and Jichang Yuan (寄 畅园) in Wuxi. Most of them are found in Suzhou and its surrounding areas.

In the following we will focus on the historical development of Suzhou gardens for illustration.

二

苏州在政治、经济、文化上，远在春秋时的吴，已经有了基础，其后两汉两晋逐渐发展。春秋时吴之梧桐园以及晋之顾辟疆园已开苏州园林的先声。六朝时，江南已为全国富庶之区。扬州、南京、苏州等处的经济基础不同，到后来形成有以商业为主，有以丝织品及手工业为主，有为官僚地主的消费城市。苏州就是以手工业为主兼为官僚地主的消费城市。

我们知道六朝以还，继以隋唐，杨广（炀帝）开运河，促使南北物资交流，唐以来因海外贸易，江南富庶视前更形繁荣。唐末中原诸省战争频繁，受到很大的破坏；可是，南唐、吴越所在范围在政治和经济上尚是小康局面，因此有余力兴建园林。宋时，苏州朱长文因吴越钱氏旧园而筑乐圃，即是一例。北宋，江南上承南唐

PART TWO

The development of Suzhou as a political, economic, and cultural center started during the reign of the Wu State in the Spring and Autumn Period of ancient China. It continued to grow through both the Han and Jin dynasties. The Parasol Garden built during the reign of the Wu State in the Spring and Autumn Period and the Garden of Gu Pijiang (顾辟疆) constructed in the Jin dynasty are the two precursors of early Suzhou gardens. The region south of Yangtze grew especially prosperous in the Six Dynasties era. The three major cities in this region are Yangzhou, Nanjing and Suzhou. In due course each of the three cities developed its economy in different ways: as a center of commerce, as a base for silk textile and the artisan handcrafts, and as a consumer town for bureaucrats. Suzhou became a site for handicraft manufacture and for consumer service for officials and land owners.

During the Sui dynasty, Emperor Yang, Yang Guang (隋炀帝，杨广) constructed the Grand Canal, thus improving the transportation of goods between the north and the south China. Since the Tang dynasty the maritime trade increased significantly, making the region south of Yangtze more prosperous than the time of the Six Dynasties. Toward the end of the Tang dynasty, while the central provinces of China were ravaged by constant warfare, the area of Southern Tang and Wuyue Kingdoms was less affected and remained stable and thriving. The status quo continued through the Northern Song dynasty. When Emperor Gaozong of the Song dynasty, Zhao Gou (宋高宗，赵构), fled south, Suzhou became the seat of Pingjiang Prefecture (平江府). This city also served as the residence of Zhao Gou during this period. Wang Huan (王�), Governor of Pingjiang Prefecture, erected pavilions and dug ponds as a garden annex in the northern part of the government building. Moreover, there was a growing trend of land ownership consolidation at the time and, as a result, there appeared numerous mansions of rich families. All these conditions favored the expansion of Suzhou gardens at the time. During the period of both the Northern and Southern Song dynasties there emerged a number of famous gardens built in the Suzhou region. Su Shunqin (苏舜钦) constructed the Garden of Canglang Ting (the Canglang Pavilion, 沧浪亭) on the site of Qian family's garden of the Wuyue Kindom period. On another site of the same Qian family's garden, Zhu Changwen (朱长文) built Lepu (乐圃). Mei Xuanyi (梅宣义) built Wumu Yuan (五亩园). Zhu Mian (朱勔) not only built and operated the garden Genyue (艮岳) for Zhao Ji (赵佶), but also constructed Tongle Yuan (同乐园) for his own enjoyment.

During the Yuan dynasty, the provinces of Jiangsu and Zhejiang continued to be a hub of wealth and prosperity. The activity in garden design and construction still ran brisk. The garden Shizilin (the Lion Forest Garden, 狮子林) was one in case. During the Ming and the Qing dynasties land ownership consolidation became even stronger. Not only was Suzhou a major manufacturing site for silk textiles and a variety of artisan handcrafts since the period of the Tang and the Song dynasties, but also it had a high concentration of land owners and bureaucrats. From this region came a significant portion of people who entered into the service of civil servants (bureaucrats) though the Keju (科举 , imperial exam) system. This city led the country in the number of Zhuangyuan (状元 , highest

吴越之旧,地方未受干戈,经济上没有受重大影响,园林兴建未辍。及赵构(高宗)南渡,苏州又为平江府治所在,赵构曾一度"驻跸"于此。王映营平江府治,其北部凿池构亭,即官衙亦附以园林。其时土地兼并已甚,豪门巨富之宅,园林建筑不言可知了。故两宋之时,苏州园林著名者,如苏舜钦就吴越钱氏故园为沧浪亭,梅宣义构五亩园,朱长文筑乐圃,而朱勔为赵佶营艮岳外,复自营同乐园,皆较为著名。元时,江浙仍为财富集中之地,故园林亦有所兴建,如狮子林,即其一例。迨入明清,土地兼并之风更甚,而苏州自唐宋以来是丝织品与各种美术工业品的产地,又为地主官僚的集中地,并且由科举登第者最多。以清一代而论,状元数字之多为全国冠。这些人年老归家,购田宅,设巨肆,除直接从土地上剥削外，再从商业上经营盘剥，以其所得大建园林以娱晚境。而手工业所生产，亦供若辈使用。其经济情况大略如此。它与隋唐洛阳、南宋吴兴、明代南京是同样情况的。

　　除了上述情况之外，在自然环境上，苏州水道纵横，湖泊罗布，随处可得泉引水，兼以土地肥沃，花卉树木易于繁滋。当地产石，除尧峰山外，洞庭东西二山所产湖石，取材便利。距苏州稍远的如江阴黄山，宜兴张公洞，镇江圌山、大岘山，句容龙潭，南京青龙山，昆山马鞍山等所产，虽不及苏州为佳，然运材亦便。而苏州诸园之选峰择石，首推湖石，因其姿态入画，具备造园条件。《宋书·戴颙传》所记"（颙）乃出居吴下。吴下士人共为筑室，聚石引水，植林开

honor from imperial exam) during the Qing dynasty. Upon retirement from the civil service, these civil servants purchased land and built residences. Profiting from land ownership as well as business operation, these people had gardens widely constructed for their enjoyment of leisure. They were also a major body of consumers of the handcrafts produced in this region. This general market condition is similar to that of Luoyang of the Sui and the Tang dynasties, Wuxing of the Southern Song dynasty, and Nanjing of the Ming dynasty.

Besides, Suzhou is endowed with the beauty of natural environment. It is situated in a region crisscrossed by waterways and dotted with numerous lakes. It is easy to find water sources and natural springs. In addition to the abundance of fresh water, the soil in this area is extremely fertile and conducive to the growth of flowers and plants. There are a number of quarries in the region providing easy access to masonry material. The famous Hushi (湖 石 , lake stone) can be found at Yaofeng Mountain (尧峰山), East Dongting (洞庭东山) and West Dongting (洞庭西山) mountains. There are also a number of accessible quarries located in neighborhoods further away from Suzhou. But the quality of stones produced there is not as fine as that found in the quarries near the city. These quarries included Huangshan Mountain of Jiangyin (江阴黄山), Zhanggong Cave of Yixing (宜兴张公洞), Chui Mountain (镇江圌山) and Daxian Mountain (镇江大岘山) of Zhenjiang, Longtan Lake at Jurong (句容龙潭), Qinglong Mountain of Nanjing (南京青龙山), and Ma'an Mountain of Kunshan (昆山马鞍山). The priority choice of masonry for garden construction in Suzhou is lake stones for the reason of their extremely picturesque shapes. The

Biography of Dai Yong in Book of Song (《宋书·戴顒 传 》) notes: "Yong came to live in the Wu region. The local scholars laid their heads together to design a house for him. They collected stones from around, channeled mountain springs to water trees planted and dug a pond after a pond. Before long, as the plants flourished, the scene of the villa became a part and parcel of the natural milieu."

In addition, Suzhou is a major center of art and scholarship in the nation. It prides itself on having an abundance of poets, writers, and painters. The scholars not only created their own ideas, but also drew wisdom from their residence advisors known as Menke (门客). It is recorded in the book *Record of Wu Region Practices* (《吴 风 录 》): "The descendants of Zhu Mian (朱 勔) live on the hill of Huqiu (虎丘). They chose the occupation of stone craftsmanship in garden construction for the high officials and royalties. The locals call them Huayuanzi (landscapers, 花园 子)." Another passage from *Miscellany on Guixin Street* (癸辛杂识) by Zhou Mi (周密) states: "The workers from Wuxing region are called rockery masons. This might be the legacy of Zhu Mian (朱 勔)." These records demonstrate the prevalence of both architects and artisans in the region. The most prominent designers since the Song dynasty were almost all from the provinces of Jiangsu and Zhejiang. Those designers worth mentioning are Yu Cheng (俞澂), Lu Dieshan (陆叠山), Ji Cheng (计成), Wen Zhenheng (文震亨), Zhang Lian (张 涟), Zhang Ran (张 然), Ye Tao (叶 洮), Li Yu (李渔), Qiu Haoshi (仇好石), and Ge Yuliang (戈 裕 良). Even today the majority of artisans specializing in rockery design come from the cities of Nanjing, Suzhou and Jinhua. Due to its long heritage in the Suzhou region, the rockery designers from Suzhou are the best known

涧，少时繁密，有若自然"，即其一例。苏州为人文荟萃之所，诗文书画人才辈出，士大夫除自出新意外，复利用了很多门客，如《吴风录》载："朱勔子孙居虎丘之麓，以种艺选石为业，游于王侯之门，俗称花园子。"又周密《癸辛杂识》云："工人特出吴兴，谓之山匠，或亦朱勔之遗风。"既有人为之策划，又兼有巧匠，故自宋以来造园家如俞澂、陆叠山、计成、文震亨、张涟、张然、叶洮、李渔、仇好石、戈裕良等，皆江浙人。今日叠石匠师出南京、苏州、金华三地，而以苏州匠师为首，是有历史根源的。但士大夫固然有财力兴建园林，然《吴风录》所载"虽闾阎下户亦饰小山盆岛为玩"，足可说明当地人民对自然的爱好了。

苏州园林在今日保存者为数最多，且亦最完整，如能全部加以整理，不啻是个花园城市。故言中国园林，当推苏州了，何怪众口之中"江南园林甲天下，苏州园林甲江南"的光荣称号呢。对于这些园林，我经过五年的调查踏勘，复曾参与修复工作，前夏与今夏又率领同济大学建筑系同学进行教学实习，主要对象是古建筑与园林，逗留时间较久。遂以测绘与摄影所得，利用拙政园、留园两个最大的园作例，略略加以说明一些苏州园林在历史上的发展与设计方面的手法，供大家研究，至于其他的一些小园林有必要述及的，亦一并包括在内。图录内所附加词句，系集宋词，对景物仅略作点缀而已。

in Jiangsu and Zhejiang areas. According to the writings in the *Record of Wu Region Practices* the art of landscaping is not just limited to the scholars who have the wealth to design and construct the garden villas, it also finds its way among "even the commoners from Lüyan (闾阎 , countryside) who still decorate their homes with small rocks". This shows the deep love of the local people for nature.

The city of Suzhou has inherited the largest and well-preserved collection of gardens within its city limits. It may well be called the city of gardens if we are able to make an inventory of the gardens still prevalent there. The gardens of Suzhou are the best amongst present day Chinese gardens. It is no wonder the gardens of Suzhou are often celebrated with the words "The gardens in the South of the Yangtze are the best in China, and the gardens of Suzhou are the best of South of the Yangtze". Over a period of five years I was able to conduct a series of survey and research on these gardens. In addition I was also involved in the restoration of several gardens. In the last two summers I came here with the students of the Department of Architecture at Tongji University to conduct onsite teaching and surveys focusing on ancient architecture and gardens. I availed myself of the long field work gathering written and photographic data for reference. The gardens Zhuozheng Yuan (the Humble Administrator's Garden, 拙 政 园) and Liuyuan (the Lingering Garden, 留 园) are used to illustrate prototypical design practices and evolution of Suzhou gardens. Other smaller gardens will be referred to wherever necessary. The verses used to describe the photos are collected or adapted from poems of the Song dynasty period. They are embellishments to the garden sceneries.

PART THREE

Zhuozheng Yuan (the Humble Administrator's Garden, 拙政园)

The Humble Administrator's Garden is located on Dongbei Jie (North East Street, 东北街), between the two city gates, Lou and Qi (娄齐二门), in the northeast corner of Suzhou city. It was constructed on the remains of Dahong Temple (大宏寺) by Wang Xianchen (王献臣) who acquired the land during Jiajing (1522-1566, 嘉靖) period of the Ming dynasty. The name "Humble Administrator" (拙政) is derived from Pan Yue's (潘岳) phrase "a humble way being an administrator" (拙者之为政).

This garden was sold to Xu family of Lizhong (里中徐氏) by Wang Xianchen's son in order to settle his gambling debt. Its ownership then fell into the hands of Chen Zhilin (陈之遴) from Haining (海宁) in the early part of the Qing dynasty. The garden became the official residence for the garrison general after Chen Zhilin was banished to a faraway outpost for penal servitude. After that, it turned into the administrative depot of military supply for local circuit.

This garden was for a time the residence of Wang Yongning (王永宁), the son-in-law of Wu Sangui (吴三桂). It was repossessed by the government after Wu Sangui's rebellion against the emperor. During the reign of Emperor Kangxi (康熙), the garden was used as the official residence of the administrator of the circuit of Suzhou, Songjiang, and Changzhou. Emperor Kangxi visited this garden during his southern tours of the empire.

The garden became divided into many small residences when the position of administrator for

三

拙政园

拙政园在娄、齐二门间的东北街。明嘉靖中（1522—1566年）王献臣因大宏寺废地营别墅，是此园的开始。"拙政"二字的由来，是用潘岳"拙者之为政"的意思。后其子以赌博负失，归里中徐氏。清初，属海宁陈之遴，陈因罪充军塞外，此园一度为驻防将军府，其后又为兵备道馆，吴三桂婿王永宁亦曾就居于此园，后没入公家。康熙初，改苏松常道新署，其时玄烨（康熙）南巡，也来游到此。苏松常道缺裁，散为民居。乾隆初，归蒋棨，易名"复园"。嘉庆中，再归海宁查世倓，复归平湖吴菘圃。迨太平天国克复苏州，又为忠王府的一部分，太平天国失败，为反动统治者所据。同治十年（1871年）改为八旗奉直会馆，仍名"拙政园"，西部归张履谦所有，易名"补园"，新中国成立后已合而为一。

1. Yaomen (side gate of the Garden)
2. Yuanxiang Tang (the Hall of Distant Fragrance)
3. Yiyu Xuan (the Bmboo Pavilion)
4. Xiaofeihong (the Small Flying Rainbow Bridge)
5. Xiangzhou (the Fragrant Isle)
6. Chengguan Lou (Clear Water Viewing Tower)
7. Yulan Tang (the Magnolia Hall)
8. Xiban Ting (West Half Pavilion) or Bieyoudongtian (Another Cave World)
9. Yiliang Ting (the Good for Both Families Pavilion)
10. Shiba Mantuoluohua Guan (the Hall of Eighteen Cmellias)
11. Sanshiliu Yuanyang Guan (the Hall of Thirty-six Pairs of Mandarin Ducks)
12. Yunwu
13. Taying Ting (the Pagoda Reflection Pavilion)
14. Liuting Ge (the Stay and Listen Pavilion)
15. Fucui Ge (the Floating Green Tower)
16. Liting (the Bamboo Hat Pavilion)
17. Yusheitongzuo Xuan ("With Whom Shall I Sit?" Pavilion), or Shanting (the Fan Pavilion)
18. Baiwenyishenzhi Zhai (the Room for Worshipping Wen and Shen, ground floor of Daoying Lou [the Tower of Reflection])
19. Jianshan Lou (the Mountain-In-View Tower)
20. Lüyi Ting (the Green Ripple Pavilion)
21. Ruin of Caihua Lou
22. Liaodi Lou
23. Daishuang Ting (the Orange Pavilion)
24. Xuexiangyunwei Ting (the Snow-Like Fragrant Prunus Mume Pavilion)
25. Hefengsimian Ting (the Pavilion in Lotus Breezes)
26. Wuzhuyouju (the Secluded Pavilion of Firmiana Simples and Bamboo)
27. Xiuqi Ting (the Paeonia Suffruticosa Pavililon)
28. Dongban Ting (East Half Pavilion) or Yihong Ting (Leaning Against Rainbow Pavilion)
29. Entrance of Pipa Yuan (Loquat Garden Court)
30. Linglong Guan (the Hall of Elegance)
31. Jiashi Ting (the Loquat Pavilion)
32. Haitangchunwu (the Malus Spectabilis Garden Court)
33. Yitingqiuyuexiaosongfeng Ting (Autumn Moon and Windy Pine Pavilion)

张宅

0   10   20   30 (m)

1. 腰门	10. 十八曼陀罗花馆	19. 见山楼	28. 东半亭（倚虹亭）
2. 远香堂	11. 三十六鸳鸯馆	20. 绿漪亭	29. 枇杷园入口
3. 南轩（倚玉轩）	12. 云坞	21. 菜花楼遗址	30. 玲珑馆
4. 小飞虹	13. 塔影亭	22. 料敌楼	31. 嘉实亭
5. 香洲	14. 留听阁	23. 待霜亭	32. 海棠春坞
6. 澂观楼	15. 浮翠阁	24. 雪香云蔚亭	33. 一庭秋月啸松风亭
7. 玉兰堂	16. 笠亭	25. 荷风四面亭	
8. 西半亭（别有洞天）	17. 与谁同坐轩（扇亭）	26. 梧竹幽居	
9. 宜两亭	18. 拜文揖沈之斋（楼上为倒影楼）	27. 绣绮亭	

拙政园平面图 | Site Plan of Zhouzheng Yuan (the Humble Administrator's Garden)

江苏省博物馆

江苏省图书馆

0 ___ 3m

拙政园中部横断面图
| Cross section of the middle part of Zhuozheng Yuan (the Humble Administrator's Garden)

0 ___ 3m

拙政园远香堂、倚玉轩、小飞虹及香洲立面图
| Elewation of Yuanxiang Tang (the Hall of Distant Fragrance), Yiyu Xuan (the Bamboo Pavilion), Xiaofeihong (the Small Flying Rainbow Bridge) and Xiangzhou (the Fragrant Isle) in Zhuozheng Yuan (the Humble Administrator's Garden)

拙政园的布局主题是以水为中心，池水面积约占总面积五分之三，主要建筑物十之八九皆临水而筑（20—21页）。文征明《拙政园记》："郡城东北界娄、齐门之间，居多隙地，有积水亘其中，稍加治，环以林木。"据此可以知道是利用原来地形而设计的，与明末计成《园冶》中《相地》一节所说"高方欲就亭台，低凹可开池沼……"的因地制宜方法相符合。故该园以水为主，实有其道理在。在苏州不但此园如此，阔街头巷的网师园，水占全园面积达五分之四，平门的五亩园亦池沼逶迤，望之弥然，莫不利用原来的地形而加以浚治的。景德路环秀山庄乾隆间蒋楫凿池得泉，名"飞雪"，亦是解决水源的好办法。

园可分中、西、东三部。中部系该园主要部分，旧时规模所存尚多；西部即张氏补园，已大加改建，然布置尚是平妥；东部为明王心一归田园居，久废，正在重建中。

circuit of Suzhou, Songjiang, and Changzhou was later eliminated. Jiang Qi (蒋 棨) brought the various parts of the garden together in early years of Emperor Qianlong's (乾 隆) reign and had it renamed as Fuyuan (复 园 , Recovered Garden). It was then sold to Zha Shitan (查 世 倓) from Haining during the reign of Emperor Jiaqing (嘉 庆). Later this garden changed hands again and became the property of Wu Songpu (吴 菘 圃) from Pinghu.

After Taiping Tianguo (Heavenly Kingdom of Great Peace, 太 平 天 国) took control of Suzhou, the garden became a part of Prince Zhong's residence (忠王府). The garden became the property of the imperial government after the rebellion of the Taiping Tianguo. It served as the venue of Baqi Clan Association (八 旗 奉 直 会 馆) starting in the tenth year of the Tongzhi (同 治) reign (1871). The garden was restored to its original name, the Humble Administrator's Garden. During this period the west section of the garden became the property of Zhang Lüqian (张 履谦) and was named Buyuan (Addition Garden, 补园). The two gardens have since been reunited into one after 1949.

The highlight of the Humble Administrator's Garden is water. Over sixty percent of the garden is covered by water. As a result of vast water coverage, eighty to ninety percent of the main buildings in the garden are built along water front (page 20-21, Site Plan of the Garden). This is documented in the article *A Record of the Humble Administrator's Garden* (《拙政园记》) by Wen Zhengming (文 征 明) in this way: "There were many marsh lands nestling in the northeastern section of the city. This is especially true for the area between the city gates Lou and Qi. Water accumulates in these areas to form natural ponds. These ponds were channeled together with little effort and lined by trees around them." It can be seen from these lines that the garden was designed based on the then existing topography.

The practice of incorporating existing topography into the design is also described by Ji Cheng（计 成）in his book *Yuanye* (*Craft of Gardens*,《园冶》) written during the late Ming dynasty. It is said in Xiangdi (Site Locating and Evaluation, 相地) section of *Yuanye*: "Pavilions and platforms should be located on high grounds, and ponds should be dug at low lands." The choice of the site for the Humble Administrator's Garden on or around water is well justified because of the readily available low lands in the area.

Incorporating existing topography into garden site planning is a common practice found in many gardens other than the Humble Administrator's Garden in Suzhou. The garden Wangshi Yuan（网师园, The Master-of-Nets Garden）at Kuojietou Xiang（阔街头巷）has eighty percent water coverage. The same is true of Wumu Yuan（五亩园）at Ping Gate（平门）, in which several small ponds were linked together to form a vast water surface. All of these gardens are invariably created by taking advantage of existing topography.

Looking for underground spring is another good way for acquiring a fresh water source. In the garden Huanxiu Shanzhuang (the Mountain Villa with Embracing Beauty, 环秀山庄) on Jingde Rd（景德路）the water source is an underground natural spring found when digging the pond. This was done by the owner Jiang Ji（蒋楫）during the reign of Emperor Qianlong（乾 隆）of the Qing dynasty. This spring was named "Flying Snow"（飞雪）by Jiang Ji.

中部远香堂为该园的主要建筑物（79 页），单檐歇山、面阔三间的四面厅。从厅内通过窗棂四望，南为小池假山：广玉兰数竿，扶疏接叶；云墙下古榆依石，幽竹傍岩；山旁修廊曲折，导游者自园外入内。似此等布置，不但在进门处可以如入山林（74 页），而坐厅南望亦有山如屏，不觉有显明的入口，这与住宅入口处置内照壁或置屏风等来作间隔的方法是采用同一手法。东望绣绮亭（83 页），西接倚玉轩（79 页），北临荷池，而隔岸雪香云蔚亭（106 页）与待霜亭（105 页）突出水面小山之上。游者坐此厅中，则一园之景可先窥其轮廓了。以此厅为中心的南北轴线上，高低起伏，主题突出。而尤以池中岛屿，环以流水，掩以丛竹，临水湖石参差，使人望去殊多不尽之意，仿佛置身于天然池沼中。从远香堂缘水东行跨倚虹桥（93 页），桥与栏皆甚低，系明代旧构。越桥达倚虹亭，亭倚墙而作，仅三面临空，故又名"东半亭"。向北达梧竹幽居（103页），亭四角攒尖，每面辟一圆拱门，此处系中部东尽头。通过二道圆拱门望池中景物，如入环中（96页）。而隔岸极远处的西半亭隐然在望，是亭内又为一圆拱门，倒映水中，所谓"别有洞天"，以通西部，亭背则北寺塔耸立云霄中，为极妙的借景。左顾远香堂、倚玉轩及香洲等，右盼两岛，前者为华丽的建筑群，后者为天然图画（95页）。刘师敦桢云："此为园林设计上运用最好的对比方法。"实际而言，东西两岸水面距离并不太大，然看去反觉深远特甚，因设计时在水面隔以梁式石桥，逶迤曲折，人们视线从水面上通过石桥才达彼岸，加以两旁一面是人工华丽的建筑，一面为天然苍翠的小山，二者之间水是修长的，自然给人们的感觉是更加深远与扩大了。而对岸老榆傍岸，垂杨临水，其间一洞窈然，楼台画出，又别有天地了。从梧竹幽居经三曲桥，

The Humble Administrator's Garden is made of three distinct parts. Its center section is the main part of the garden. This section contains the majority of the original designs that have survived over the years. The west section is the portion of garden that used to be Buyuan (Addition Garden, 补园) of Zhang family. This section has received many major modifications but maintained its original style. These changes do not diminish the glamour of a well designed garden. The east section was Guitianyuanju (Retreat House, 归田园居) of Wang Xinyi's (王心一) during the Ming dynasty, which has long been neglected, and is now being restored.

Yuanxiang Tang (the Hall of Distant Fragrance, 远香堂) (page 79) is the principal building in the center section of the garden, with a four-sided three-bay-wide hall, and a single eave gable-on-hip roof (单檐歇山). Looking south from the hall one enjoys a view of a small pond with rockery. There is a lush green shade provided by several clusters of magnolia. An old elm tree stands by the rock nearby an undulating wall (云墙). A line of dark green bamboo hugs the rockery. The slender winding veranda follows the curve of the hill rocks. It leads the visitor into the garden. This type of site planning not only creates an impression of entering a natural forest (page 74) for the visitors, but also effectively hides the garden entrance for people looking south from the main hall by using the rockery as a natural screen. This design technique is similar to the use of Zhaobi (screen wall, 照壁) or Pingfeng (screen, 屏风) at the entrance of a residence.

Sitting inside the Hall of Distant Fragrance and looking at north, one can get a glimpse of major sceneries of the whole center section of the garden, with Xiuqi Ting (Paeonia Suffruticosa Pavilion, 绣绮亭 , page 83) to the east, Yiyu Xuan (Bamboo Pavilion, 倚玉轩 , page 79) on the west side, a large lotus pond bordering the north side, as well as two pavilions atop islets across the pond, named Xuexiangyunwei Ting (Snow-Like Fragrant Prunus Mume Pavilion, 雪香云蔚亭 , page 106) and Daishuang Ting (Orange Pavilion, 待霜亭 , page 105). Along the north-to-south axis of the Hall of Distant Fragrance the garden's profile goes up and down with accentuating motifs. In particular, the islets in the pond are surrounded with flowing water, veiled by dwarf bamboo, and adorned by lime stones along the jagged shore. The whole view stretches one's boundless imagination as if one had found oneself in a true natural scene of lake.

Strolling along the waterside trail eastward from the Hall of Distant Fragrance takes one to the bridge Yihong Qiao (Leaning Against Rainbow Bridge, 倚虹桥 , page 93). This bridge is a part of the original Ming dynasty construction. It is characterized by the low balustrade and close proximity of the bridge surface to water surface. After crossing the bridge one arrives at the pavilion Yihong Ting (Leaning Against Rainbow Pavilion, 倚虹亭). This pavilion is built with its east side against a wall and the other three sides to open terrain. Therefore, it is also called East Half Pavilion (东半亭).

The passage northward from the Leaning Against Rainbow Pavilion leads to the Pavilion Wuzhuyouju (Secluded Pavilion of Firmiana Simplex and Bamboo 梧竹幽居 , page 103). This is a pavilion with a pyramid-shaped roof and a ring-shaped gate on each of its four sides. Here is the east end of the center section of the garden.

Looking at the west of the garden through the two ring-shaped gates one gets an extraordinary view of the beauty around the pool (page 96), with a dimly visible sight of the West Half Pavilion (西半亭) located far away on the opposite side of the garden across the pond. The West Half Pavilion is well known as Bieyoudongtian (Another Cave World, 别有洞天) which refers to the moon gate in this pavilion since this moon gate leads into the west section of the garden.

At the Secluded Pavilion of Firmiana Simplex and Bamboo, one can see the reflection of the gate "Another Cave World" in the water, and the pagoda Beisi Ta (North Temple Pagoda, 北寺塔) rising sheer into the sky behind the West Half Pavilion. This is a spectacular use of the scene borrowing (借景) technique. Besides there is a sharp contrast presented to the viewer at this vantage point (page 95). The left side of the pool unfolds a group of elaborate buildings including the Hall of Distant Fragrance, the Bamboo Pavilion, and Xiangzhou (Fragrant Isle, 香洲). On the right side lie two small islets in a totally natural milieu. "This is the best use of contrast in a garden design," as noted by Master Liu Dunzhen (刘敦桢). As a matter of fact, the physical distance between the east and the west sides of the pond is not particularly large. But the visual effect of the design provides an illusion of depth. This is partly due to the construction of a winding stone clapper bridge across the pond. One's sight lingers on the bridge before reaching the west shore. On the other hand, the strip of water between the north and the south shores is slender, and the magnificent buildings on the south contrast wonderfully with the natural verdant hills on the north. All these give people a profound feeling of depth and extension. With aged elm standing by the shore, swaying

小径分歧，屈曲循道登山，达巅为待霜亭（105 页）。亭六角，翼然出丛竹间，向东襟带绿漪亭（99 页），西则复与长方形的雪香云蔚亭（106 页）相呼应。此岛平面为三角形，与雪香云蔚亭一岛椭圆形者有别，二者之间一溪相隔。溪上覆以小桥（110 页），其旁幽篁丛出，老树斜依，而清流涓涓宛若与树上流莺相酬答，至此顿忘尘嚣了。自雪香云蔚亭下，便到荷风四面亭（142 页）。亭亦六角，居三路之交点，前者皆以曲桥相贯，前通倚玉轩而后达见山楼及别有洞天。经曲廊名"柳荫路曲"者（124 页）达见山楼（112 页）。楼为重檐歇山顶，以假山构成云梯可导至楼层。是楼地位居中部西北之角，因此登楼远望，其至四周距离较大，所见景物亦远，如转眼北眺，则城隈景物，又瞬入眼帘了。此种手法在中国园林中最为常用，如中由吉巷半园用五边形亭，狮子林用扇面亭（287 页），皆置于角

willow leaning onto the water, a new cluster of pavilions and halls looming through an elegant gate in between, what catches one's eye is another wonderland on the opposite bank.

Walking along the passage westward from the Secluded Pavilion of Firmiana Simplex and Bamboo and crossing the Sanqu Qiao (the Three Fold Zigzag Bridge, 三曲桥) one descends on a small triangle shaped islet. Taking the winding trail up hill one arrives at a hexagonal shaped pavilion nestling among dwarf bamboos at the peak, which is named Daishuang Ting (Orange Pavilion, 待霜亭 , page 105). To its east and across the water is the Pavilion Lüyi Ting (Green Ripple Pavilion, 绿漪亭 , page 99). On the west it is matched by the Snow-Like Fragrant Prunus Mume Pavilion (page 106), which is a rectangular shaped pavilion located on an elliptical shaped islet. A small bridge across a small creek connects the two islets (page 110). Enchanted by aged trees leaning in a bamboo grove, clear stream gurgling and orioles twittering in the arbor brush, one feels a sudden isolation from the mundane world.

The trail winding down from the Snow-Like Fragrant Prunus Mume Pavilion leads to the Pavilion Hefengsimian Ting (Pavilion in Lotus Breezes, 荷风四面亭 , page 142). This is another hexagonal shaped pavilion. It is at the confluence point of three passages, with connecting zigzag bridges on two of the passages. The way forward heads for the Bamboo Pavilion, while the way backward brings one to Jianshan Lou (Mountain-In-View Tower, 见山楼) and "Another Cave World" through the winding veranda Liuyinluqu (A Winding Way with Willow Shades, 柳荫路曲 , page 124). The Mountain-In-View Tower (page 112) is a two-storey building with a double eave gable-on-hip roof (重檐歇山顶). Its second storey is reached via a staircase formed by rockery on the exterior. This building is located on the northwest corner of the center section of the garden. It is well separated from other structures in all dirctions, providing a wide-angled view from the top of the building. The whole city comes into focus when looking northward.

This type of vantage viewpoints can be found in many Chinese gardens. For example the pentagonal shaped pavilion built in Banyuan (Half Garden, 半园) at Zhongyouji Xiang (中由吉巷), and Shanmian Ting (Fan Pavilion, 扇面亭 , page 287) found in Shizilin (the Lion Forest Garden, 狮子林) are both located on high peaks in the corner of the gardens.

Due to the large size and expansive water surface of the Humble Administrator's Garden, such a two-storey tower built in it does not look overly tall. What's more, its reflection in the limpid water is a welcome addition to the scenery. However, in designing a two-storey building in a garden due attention should be paid to its architrave arrangement at elevation. One should adopt more horizontal lines running in parallel to the water surface in order to achieve a better consistency.

The Fragrant Isle is traditionally known as a land boat, a buiding formed in the shape of a boat though it cannot float as a boat on water (page 126-129). There is a large mirror lodged in the bay of the building. When viewed from the Bamboo Pavilion, one cannot tell whether one sees a true subject or a reflection in the mirror. It also gives a sense of depth to a relatively shallow area. The upper part of the two-storey structure of Fragrant Isle, which is called Chengguan Lou (澄观楼 ,

间略高的山巅。至于此园面积较大，而积水弥漫，建一重楼，但望去不觉高耸凌云，而水间倒影清澈，尤增园林景色。然在设计时应注意其立面线脚，宜多用横线，盖与水面取得平行，以求统一。香洲俗呼"旱船"，形似船而不能行水者（126—129页），入舱置一大镜，故从倚玉轩西望，镜中景物，真幻莫辨。楼上名澄观楼，亦宜眺远。向南为得真亭（138页），内置一镜，命意与前同。是区水面狭长，上跨石桥名"小飞虹"（133页），将水面划分为二；其南水榭三间，名"小沧浪"，亦跨水上，又将水面再度划分；二者之下皆空，不但不觉其局促，反觉面积扩大，空灵异常，层次渐多了。人们视线从小沧浪穿过小飞虹及一庭秋月啸松风亭（133页、137页），水面极为辽阔，而荷风四面亭倒影、香洲侧影、见山楼角皆先后入眼中（134页），真有从小窥大，顿觉开朗的样子。枇杷园在远香堂东南，以云墙相隔，通月门（81页），则嘉实亭与玲珑馆分列于前，复自月门回望雪香云蔚亭，如在环中，此为最好的对景（80页）。我们坐园中，垣外高槐亭台，移置身前，为极好的借景。园内用鹅子石铺地，雅洁异常。惜沿墙假山修时已变更原形，而云墙上部无收头，转折又略嫌生硬（81页）。从玲珑馆旁曲廊至海棠春坞（89页），屋仅面阔二间，阶前古树一木，海棠一树，佳石一二。近屋以短廊，漏窗外亭阁水石，隐约在望（90—91页）。其环境表面上看来是封闭的，而实际是处处通畅，面面玲珑，置身其间，便感到密处有疏，小处现大，可见设计手法运用的巧妙了。

　　西部与中部原来是不分开的，后来一园划分为二，始用墙间隔，如今又合而为一，因此墙上开了漏窗。当其划分时，西部欲求有整体性，于是不得不在小范围内加工，沿水的墙边

Clear Water Viewing Tower), is in an advantageous position for enjoying faraway scenery.

To the south of the Fragrant Isle is the Pavilion Dezhen Ting (True Nature Pavilion, 得真亭, page 138), in which there is also a mirror that creates similar effect of illusion. In this area there is a narrow strip of water. The stone bridge Xiaofeihong (Small Flying Rainbow Bridge, 小飞虹, page 133) crosses over the water surface and breaks it into two parts. To the south of the bridge, a three bay pavilion Xiaocanglang (Small Canglang, 小沧浪) perches over the water and further divides the water surface. With open spaces beneath the bridge and pavilion, one does not feel any constraint in this narrow area. Instead, the structural arrangement gives people a free and unrestrained feeling.

Looking from the Small Canglang and through the Small Flying Rainbow Bridge and the Pavilion Yitingqiuyuexiaosongfeng Ting (Autumn Moon and Windy Pine Pavilion, 一庭秋月啸松风亭, page 133 and 137), one has a panoramic view of a large expanse of water with the reflection of the Pavilion in Lotus Breeze in it, the profile of the Fragrant Isle as well as the Mountain-In-View Tower afar (page 134). This multiple level scenery gives a sense of looking at a grand view through a small portal, and cheers up the viewer with its clear open space.

Pipa Yuan (Loquat Garden Court, 枇杷园) lies on the southeast side of the Hall of Distant Fragrance. It is separated by an undulating wall from the rest of the garden. There is a moon gate connecting the two sections (page 81). Jiashi Ting (Loquat Pavilion, 嘉实亭) and Linglong Guan (Hall of Elegance, 玲珑馆) are both situated in the front portion of the Court. Sitting in the Courtyard and looking at the Snow-Like Fragrant Prunus Mume Pavilion through the moon gate one has the impression that the pavilion is embedded in a ring. This is among the best in paired scenery (对 景 , page 80). It seems as if we were sitting within a painting, with the tall scholar tree and pavilions by the low wall fore-grounded indeed. This is an extremely good use of scene borrowing (借 景). The courtyard ground is paved with cobblestones in an elegant fashion. Unfortunately the rockery along the wall has lost its original shape during reconstruction; the upper part of the undulating wall lacks the traditional ending, and the turn in the wall lacks finesse (page 81).

A winding veranda on the side of the Hall of Elegance leads to Haitangchunwu (Malus Spectabilis Garden Court, 海 棠 春 坞 , page 89). This is only a two-bay-wide building . Standing by the steps are an aged tree, a crabapple, and some scattered pieces of rockery; surrounding the Court is a veranda; veiled behind the tracery windows are pavilions and bowers, water and rock (page 90-91). With such careful arrangements in a closed and confined space, the Court looks delicate and elegant at every point, and spacious and smooth in every direction. This demonstrates the ingenuity of Chinese garden design, which enables sparsity artistically spaced with density and *multum* in *parvo*.

A wall was built between the west and center sections when the Humble Administrator's Garden was split to two gardens. Tracery windows were added in the wall after these two sections were united. Some minor modifications had been made in the west section when it was split out, in order to create an independent entity. A winding veranda over the water was built along the wall.

就构了水廊，廊复有曲折高低的变化，人行其上，宛若凌波（156页），是苏州诸园中之游廊极则。三十六鸳鸯馆与十八曼陀罗花馆系鸳鸯厅（172页），为西部主要建筑物，外观为歇山顶，面阔三间，内用卷棚四卷（175页），四隅各加暖阁，其形制为国内孤例。此厅体积似乎较大，其因实由于西部划分后，欲成为独立的单位，此厅遂为主要建筑部分，在需要上不能不建造，但碍于地形，于是将前部空间缩小，后部挑出水中，虽然解决了地位安顿问题，但卒使水面变狭与对岸之山距离太近。陆地缩小，而本身又觉与全园不称，当然是美中不足处。此厅为主人宴会与顾曲之处，因此在房屋结构上除运用卷棚顶以增加演奏效果外，其四隅之暖阁，既解决进出时风击问题，复可利用为宴会时仆从听候之处，演奏时暂作后台之用，设想上是相当周到。内部的装修精致与留听阁同为苏州少见的。至于初春

十八曼陀罗花馆看宝珠山茶花，夏日
三十六鸳鸯馆看鸳鸯于荷藻间，宜乎
南北各置一厅了。对岸为浮翠阁，八
角二层，登阁可鸟瞰全园，惜太高峻，
与环境不称。其下隔溪小山上置二亭，
即笠亭（178页）与扇亭（181页），
亭皆不大，盖山较低小，不得不使然。
扇亭位于临流转角，因地而设，宜于
闲眺，故颜其额为"与谁同坐轩"。
亭下为修长流水，水廊缘边以达倒影
楼（160页）。楼为歇山顶，高二层，
与六角攒尖的宜两亭（164页）遥遥
相对，皆倒影水中，互为对景。鸳鸯
厅西部之溪流中置塔影亭（189页），
它与其北的留听阁（186页）同样在
狭长的水面二尽头，而外观形式亦相
仿佛，不过地位视前二者为低，布局
与命意还是相同。塔影亭南原为补园
入口以通张宅，今已封闭。东部久废，
刻在重建中，从略。

The veranda rises and falls while snaking along the water, making people feel like treading the water waves while walking through the veranda (page 156). This is the best touring veranda design amongst all found in Suzhou gardens.

The Sanshiliu Yuanyang Guan (Hall of Thirty-six pairs of Mandarin Ducks, 三十六鸳鸯馆) and Shiba Mantuoluohua Guan (Hall of Eighteen Camellias 十八曼陀罗花馆) is a twin hall (page 172). This is the main structure in the west section, three bays wide, with a gable-on-hip roof at exterior. But there is no roof ridge seen in the interior. Instead, four fold arc ceilings (卷棚四卷, page 175) are used. Additionally, there are four rooms with individual pyramid roofs at the four corners of the building. As a result its design is unique in the country.

This twin hall was built when the west section was split out, out of the need of a main structure in a stand-alone garden. In order to fit such a big hall into a constrained space, it was necessary to downsize the front portion of the hall and extend the rear of the hall over the water. Consequently, the water surface is reduced. The short distance to the hills across the pond and the limited clearing around the building makes the hall inconsistent with the rest of the garden to a certain degree. These are the defects in an otherwise perfect design.

This hall was used by the owner to dine and entertain guests. The special interior roof structure enhances its acoustic effects. The rooms at four corners provide not only a way to reduce the wind rush while people entering and leaving the hall, but also a space for the servants in waiting on call, or for the performers as a temporary backstage. The designer has taken all things into consideration when designing the structure. Its interior decorations along with those found in another building, Liuting Ge (Stay And Listen Pavilion, 留听阁) are among the most ornate found in Suzhou. The Hall of Eighteen Camellias is an ideal spot for enjoying camellia flowers during early sping. And in the Hall of Thirty-six Pairs of Mandarin Ducks watching mandarin ducks playing amongst the lotus is a favorite pastime during summer. It is fitting to have these two halls with one facing the south and the other the north.

The Fucui Ge (Floating Green Tower, 浮翠阁) sits aside the water from the twin hall. It is a two storey octagonal structure. A bird's eye view of the garden is provided from the top of the building. It is unfortunate the structure is un-proportionately tall and does not fit in scale with the rest of the garden. Down from the Floating Green Tower and across a creek, two small pavilions are crouching on a small hill. They are Liting (Bamboo Hat Pavilion, 笠亭 , page 178) and Shanting (Fan Pavilion, 扇亭 , page 181). Fan Pavilion is also called "With Whom Shall I Sit?" Pavilion (与谁同坐轩). Being located at a bend of a slender stream, this Pavilion fits for leisure and relaxation.

Walking northward along the winding veranda over the water one reaches Daoying Lou (Tower of Reflection, 倒影楼 , page 160). This is a two storey building with a gable-on-hip roof. Sitting opposite to its south is a hexagonal pyramid-shape roofed pavilion, Yiliang Ting (Good for Both Families Pavilion, 宜两亭 , page 164). The beautiful reflections of both buildings in the water form a perfect scene pairing.

Another scene pairing of similar type can be found to the west of the twin hall. In this case, on the south is the pavilion Taying Ting (Pagoda Reflection Pavilion, 塔影亭 , page 189) while on the north is the Stay and Listen Pavilion (page 186). Both sets of building and pavilion pairs are astride a narrow body of water. The exterior shapes of the two pairs are extremely similar although the latter pair is located on lower ground than the former.

When the west section was split off from the garden, a new entrance was opened at the south side of the Pagoda Reflection Pavilion, which serves also as a passage to Zhang's residence.

The east side of the garden has long since fallen to disrepair. Its rebuilding is being planned, and will not be discussed here. (Note by Translator: The east section has been rebuilt and opened to public. Indeed, the entrance to the garden is now in the east section.)

留园

在阊门外留园路，明中叶为徐泰时东园，清嘉庆年间（约1800年）刘恕重建，称"寒碧山庄"，又名"刘园"。园中旧有十二峰，为太湖石之上选。光绪二年（1876年）间归盛康，易名"留园"。园占地五十市亩（约33公顷），面积为苏州诸园之冠（36—37页）。

是园可划分为东、西、中、北四部。中部以水为主，环绕山石楼阁，贯以长廊小桥。东部以建筑为主，列大型厅堂，参置轩斋，间列立峰斧劈，在平面上曲折多变。西部以大假山为主，漫山枫林，亭榭一二，南面环以曲水，仿晋人武陵桃源，是区与中部以云墙相隔，红叶出粉墙之上，望之若云霞，为中部最好的借景。北部旧构已毁，今又重辟，平淡无足观，从略。

中部：入园门经二小院至绿荫

Liuyuan (Lingering Garden, 留园)

The Lingering Garden is located on Liuyuan Road just outside of city gate Chang (阊 门). It was originally known as East Garden of Xu Taishi (徐 泰 时) during the Ming dynasty. During the reign of Emperor Jiaqing (嘉 庆) of the Qing dynasty (circa 1800) this garden was rebuilt by Liu Shu (刘恕). It was called Hanbi Shanzhuang (寒 碧 山 庄) at this time, but was commonly known as the Garden of Liu. There were twelve rockery peaks in this garden which were crafted from the best lake stones found in the Taihu Lake (太湖). This garden then became the possession of Sheng Kang (盛康) in 2nd year of Emperor Guangxu's (光 绪) reign (1876) and renamed as Lingering Garden. Occupying an area of fifty Mu (circa 33 ha), it is the largest garden in Suzhou (page 36-37).

This garden is divided into four parts, i.e. center, east, west, and north in light of their respective locations. The center section consists of a large ponal surrounded by hills, rockeries, and buildings, which are stringed together by a series of verandas and bridges. The east section features its variety of buildings. In this part large and magnificent halls are accentuated by small studies and lined by rugged rockeries, resulting in a layout full of variation. The west section is mainly a man-made hill covered by a maple tree grove and dotted with a few pavilions. The south side of the hill is ringed by water to imitate the Peach Blossom Spring fabricated by Tao Yuanming of the Jin dynasty (晋人武陵桃源). This section is partitioned from the center section by an undulating wall. The red leaves poking above the pale white walls look like red clouds sailing from distant sky. It forms the best borrowing scene (借

景) in the center section. The structures currently found in the north part are all recent reconstruction. These buildings lack character in design. This section will not be discussed in detail.

Center Section: Entering the garden's front gate and passing through two small courtyards, one arrives at Lüyin (Green Shade Pavilion, 绿荫, page 197). Through the tracery windows on the north side, one has a dim view of the hills and buildings in the garden. Going westward one reaches the main building of the center section, Hanbi Shanfang (Hanbi [Be imbued with the green] Mountain Villa 涵碧山房, page 203). This is a three bays wide building, with a gabled roof with flushing purlins (硬山造). On its south side is a small courtyard with a peony flower bed in the center while on its north side is a terrace bordering a lotus pond. Abutting against the Villa on the east is Mingse Lou (Pellucid Tower, 明瑟楼, page 205). This is an ornate two storey building with a single sided gable-on-hip roof (单面歇山顶, page 203, upper). The second story can be reached via a scaling stair.

Continuing west from the Hanbi Mountain Villa and climbing up a veranda, one ascends to Wenmuxixiang Xuan (Osmanthus Fragrance Pavilion, 闻木樨香轩, page 209). This location affords a panoramic view of the center section and the surrounding areas. On the east side there is a spectacular array of buildings such as Quxi Lou (Winding Stream Tower, 曲溪楼), Xilou (Western Tower, 西楼), Qingfengchi Guan (Refreshing Breeze Pavilion by the Lake, 清风池馆), Jigudegengchu (Study of Enlightenment, 汲古得绠处) and Yuancui Ge (Distant Green Tower, 远翠阁). These buildings, high or low and nestling

（197 页），自漏窗北望，隐约见山池楼阁片段，向西达涵碧山房三间（203 页），硬山造，为中部的主要建筑，前为小院，中置牡丹台，后临荷池。其左明瑟楼倚涵碧山房而筑（205 页），高二层，屋顶用单面歇山（203 页），外观玲珑，由云梯可导至二层。复从涵碧山房西折上爬山游廊，登闻木樨香轩（209 页），坐此可周视中部，尤其东部曲溪楼、西楼、清风池馆、汲古得绠处及远翠阁等，参差前后，高下相呼的诸楼阁掩映于古木奇石之间。南面则廊屋花墙，水阁互联，而明瑟楼微突水面，涵碧山房之凉台再突水面，层层布局，略作环抱之势，楼前清水一池，倒影历历在目。自闻木樨香轩向北东折经游廊达远翠阁，是阁位于中部东北角（221 页），其用意与拙政园见山楼相同，不过一在水，一在陆，又紧依东部，隔花墙为东部最好的借景（216 页）。小蓬莱

留园平面图 | Site plan of Liuyuan (the Lingering Garden) in Suzhou

0   10   20 (m)

1. 门厅	17. 还我读书处
2. 古木交柯	18. 揖峰轩
3. 绿荫	19. 林泉耆硕之馆
4. 涵碧山房	20. 亦不二亭
5. 凉台	21. 伫云庵
6. 明瑟楼	22. 冠云楼
7. 闻木樨香轩	23. 冠云亭
8. 可亭	24. 冠云台
9. 远翠阁	25. 浣云沼
10. 小蓬莱	26. 东园一角亭
11. 濠濮亭	27. 佳晴喜雨快雪之亭
12. 曲溪楼	28. 陈列馆
13. 西楼	29. 至乐亭
14. 清风池馆	30. 舒啸亭
15. 五峰仙馆	31. 活泼泼地
16. 汲古得绠处	32. 水阁

1. Menting (entrance hall)
2. Gumujiaoke (the Intertwined Old Trees)
3. Lüyin (the Green Shade Pavilion)
4. Hanbi Shanfang (the Hanbi [Be imbued with the green] Mountain Villa)
5. Liangtai (Terrace at the north of Hanbi Shanfang [The Hanbi (Be imbued with the green) Mountain Villa])
6. Mingse Lou (the Pellucid or the Pure Freshness Tower)
7. Wenmuxixiang Xuan (the Osmanthus Fragrance Pavilion)
8. Keting (the Passable Pavilion)
9. Yuancui Ge (the Distant Green Tower)
10. Xiaopenglai (the Small Fairy Isle)
11. Haopu Ting (the Haopu Pavilion)
12. Quxi Lou (the Winding Stream Tower)
13. Xilou (Western Tower)
14. Qingfengchi Guan (the Refreshing Breeze Pavilion by the Lake)
15. Wufengxian Guan (the Celestial Hall of Five Peaks)
16. Jigudegengchu (the Study of Enlightenment)
17. Huanwodushuchu (the Return-to-Read Study)
18. Yifeng Xuan (the Worshipping Stone Pavilion)
19. Linquanqishuozhi Guan (the Old Hermit Scholars' Hall)
20. Yibu'er Ting
21. Zhuyun'an (the Standing Cloud Hut)
22. Guanyun Lou (the Cloud-Capped Tower)
23. Guanyun Ting (the Cloud-Capped Pavilion)
24. Guanyun Tai (the Cloud-Capped Terrace)
25. Huanyunzhao (the Cloud Bathing Pond)
26. A pavilion at the corner of eastern section
27. Jiaqingxiyukuaixuezhi Ting (the Good-For-Farming Pavilion)
28. Exhibition Hall
29. Zhile Ting (the Delightful Pavilion)
30. Shuxiao Ting (the Free Roaring Pavilion)
31. Huopopodi (the Place of Liveliness)
32. Shuige

0   5   10 (m)

留园横断面图
| Cross section of Liuyuan (the Lingering Garden)

0   5   10 (m)

留园纵断面图
| Longitudinal section of Liuyuan (the Lingering Garden)

宛在水中央，濠濮亭（223页）列其旁，皆几与水平，如此对比，容易显山之峻与楼之高了。曲溪楼（224页）底层西墙皆列砖框、漏窗，游者至此，感觉处处邻虚，移步换影，眼底如画。而尤其举首西望，秋时枫林如醉，衬托于云墙之后，其下高低起伏若波然，最令人依恋不已。北面为假山，可亭（214页）六角出假山之上，其后则为长廊了。

东部主要建筑物有二：其一五峰仙馆（楠木厅，230页），面阔五间，系硬山造，内部装修陈设，精致雅洁，为江南旧式厅堂布置之上选（232页）。其前后左右皆有大小不等的院子，前后二院皆列假山，人坐厅中仿佛面对岩壑，然此法为明计成所不取，《园冶》云："人皆厅前掇山，环堵中耸起高高三峰，排列于前，殊为可笑。"此厅列五峰于前，似觉太挤，了无生趣。而计成认为在这种情况下

among or snuggling against trees and rocks, enhance each other's beauty like a charm.

On the south side of the Osmanthus Fragrance Pavilion, pavilions and towers adjoin verandas and latticed window walls one after another along the water. The Pellucid Tower juts out to the water slightly, while the north terrace of the Hanbi Mountain Villa protrudes into the pond even further. This layered arrangement seems embosoming the water in the center and leaves a beautiful reflection of scene in the lucid pond.

The veranda north of the Osmanthus Fragrance Pavilion turns eastward at the north end of the garden and leads to the Distant Green Tower located in the northeast corner of the center section (page 221). This tower serves the same purpose as the Mountain-In-View Tower in the Humble Administrator's Garden, though this building sits on land while the other by the water. Being located next to the east section of the garden and separated only by a wall adorned with latticed windows, the Distant Green Tower provides the east section with a magnificent borrowed scene (page 216).

Standing in the middle of the water is Xiaopenglai (Small Fairy Isle, 小蓬莱), with Haopu Ting (Haopu Pavilion, 濠濮亭, page 223) across the pond. Both of them are at the water level, which provides a significant contrast in height to the nearby hills and towers. The west wall of ground floor of the Wingding Stream Tower (page 224) is lined with brick-framed tracery windows . Picturesque views through these widows keep varying while walking along the wall, creating fantastic and kaleidoscopic sceneries. In particular, when autumn comes, dark red maple leaves on the hill of the west section ebb and flow behind the undulating wall, making everyone thrilled.

Returning to Pellucid Tower and looking north, the hexagon shaped pavilion Keting (Passable Pavilion, 可亭, page 214) stands atop the hill across the lotus pond, with the long veranda leading towards the Distant Green Tower at the back.

East Section: There are two major buildings in the east section. The first building is Wufengxian Guan (Celestial Hall of Five Peaks, 五峰仙馆、or Hall of Nanmu, page 230). This is a five-bay wide hall with a gable roof with flushing purlins (硬山造). The interior decoration of this building is especially delicate and ornate (page 232). It is one of the best old style halls in the region south of Yangtze. The courtyards on all four sides vary in size. There are rockeries in both the front and the back courtyards, which makes one feel as if he is facing cliffs when sitting in the hall. This design was not appreciated by Ji Cheng of the Ming dynasty. He noted in the book *Yuanye* (*Craft of Gardens*, 《园冶》): "Everybody wants to build rockeries in front of a hall. Having three high peaks stand and line up in a limited courtyard is funny indeed." In the Celestial Hall of Five Peaks, there are five rockeries in the front yard, making the court look overly crowded and devoid of lively interest. Under these conditions Ji Cheng also said that one should "either put only small and exquisite rockeries amongst fine trees, or embed the rockeries within the wall, or plant some ivy or grass atop rockeries, in order to enhance perception of depth". This would be a more viable design practice in my own opinion. In the backyard, there is a limpid spring in front

应该是"以予见或有嘉树稍点玲珑石块，不然墙中嵌埋壁岩，或顶植卉木垂萝，似有深境也"。我觉得这办法妥善多了。后部小山前有清泉一泓，境界至静，惜源头久没，泉呈时涸时有之态。山后沿墙绕以回廊，可通左右前后，游者至此，偶一不慎，方向莫辨。在此小院中左眺远翠阁，则隔院楼台又炯然在目，使人益觉该园之宽大了。其旁汲古得绠处，小屋一间，紧依五峰仙馆，入内则四壁皆虚，中部景物又复现眼前。其与五峰仙馆相关联处的小院中植梧桐一树，望之亭亭如盖，此小空间的处理是极好的手法。还我读书处与揖峰轩都是两个小院，在五峰仙馆的左邻，是介于与林泉耆硕之馆中间，为两大建筑物中之过渡。小院绕以回廊，间以砖框，院中安排佳木修竹，萱草片石，都是方寸得宜，楚楚有致，使人有静中生趣之感，充分发挥了小院落的设计手法

249 页），而游者至此往往相失。由揖峰轩向东为林泉耆硕之馆，俗呼"鸳鸯厅"，装修陈设极尽富丽（252 页），屋面阔五间，单檐歇山造，前后二厅，内部各施卷棚（252 页、254 页），主要一面向北，大木梁架用"扁作"，有雕刻，南面用"圆作"，无雕刻。厅北对浣云沼，冠云（256 页）、岫云（269 页）、瑞云（268 页）三峰以及冠云亭、冠云楼。三峰为明代旧物，苏州最大的湖石。冠云峰后侧为冠云亭（257 页、265 页），亭六角，倚玉兰花下。向北登云梯上冠云楼，虎丘塔影，阡陌平畴，移置窗前了。伫云庵与冠云台位于沼之东西。从冠云台入月门乃佳晴喜雨快雪之亭，亭内楠木槅扇六扇，雕刻甚精，为吴中装修之极品（270 页）。惜是亭面西，难免受阳光风露之损伤。东园一角系新辟，山石平淡无奇，不足与旧构相颉颃了。

of the rockery, which provides an extremely quiet environment. It is unfortunate the spring has lost its source, and become intermittent. A veranda runs along the walls of this backyard. This veranda can lead to various directions and hence might disorient a person arriving at this point for the first time. The Distant Green Tower is clearly visible when looking left from this backard. The yonder pavilion further demonstrates spaciousness of the garden .

The building Jigudegengchu (Study of Enlightenment, 汲古得绠处) is a one bay room adjacent to the Celestial Hall of Five Peaks. This structure has open void on all four walls, which provides a view of the sceneries in the center section. A flourishing umbrella shaped Chinese parasol tree stands erect in its courtyard adjoining the Celestial Hall of Five Peaks. This is a case of ingenious treatment of small space in design.

The buildings Huanwodushuchu (the Return-to-Read Study, 还我读书处) and Yifeng Xuan (the Worshipping Stone Pavilion, 揖峰轩) are both small courts on the east side of the Celestial Hall of Five Peaks. These two buildings serve as a transition in the space between the Celestial Hall of Five Peaks and Linquanqishuozhi Guan (the Old Hermit Scholars' Hall, 林泉耆硕之馆). Here one can observe the full applications of small court design (page 240-249). These small courts are surrounded by verandas and separated by hollow walls with brick framed windows. Inside the courts are arrayed fine trees accompanied with slender bamboos, as well as day lilies around slabs of rockery. All things here are well matched in size and in space, making the layout of the courts neat and tidy. One draws a lot of fun and enjoyment from these still objects and is often reluctant to depart.

The building east of the Worshipping Stone Pavilion is the second major building in the east section, the Old Hermit Scholars' Hall (林泉耆硕之馆). The decoration in this building is extremely elaborate and rich (page 252). It is a five-bay-wide twin hall with a single eave gable-on-hip roof at exterior and two separate arc ceilings for each hall in the interior (page 252 and 254). The main hall faces north. Its main beam is made of flat wood decorated with carved patterns. In the south hall, the main beam is a round lumber without any carved decoration.

The north hall of the Old Hermit Scholars' Hall faces Huanyunzhao (the Cloud Bathing Pond, 浣 云 沼) as well as Guanyun Ting (the Cloud-Capped Pavilion, 冠云亭) and Guanyun Lou (the Cloud-Capped Tower, 冠 云 楼). Here stand the three most famous rockeries in Suzhou: Guanyun Feng (the Cloud-Capped Peak, 冠云峰, page 256), Xiuyun Feng (the Mountainous Cloud Peak, 岫云峰, page 269), and Ruiyun Feng (the Auspicious Cloud Peak, 瑞 云 峰, page 268). There three peaks are a part of the original design of the Ming dynasty. They are the largest lake rockeries ever found in Suzhou.

The Cloud-Capped Pavilion is a hexagonal shaped pavilion located on the side of the Cloud-Capped Peak (page 275 and 265). There are magnolia trees planted around the Pavilion. By climbing a scaling stair at the north side of the Pavilion, one ascends to the Cloud-Capped Tower. At this place one enjoys an open view beyond the garden. The vast cultivated fields crisscrossed with footpaths and the dimly-visible pagoda image of distant Huqiu (the Tiger Hill，虎丘), all come in sight at the window.

The buildings Zhuyun'an (the Standing Cloud Hut, 伫云庵) and Guanyun Tai (the Cloud-Capped Terrace, 冠云台) are located on the east and the west sides of the Cloud Bathing Pond, respectively. The Jiaqingxiyukuaixuezhi Ting (the Good-For-Farming Pavilion、佳 晴 喜 雨 快 雪 之 亭) is accessible from the Cloud-Capped Terrace through a moon gate. In the Good-For-Farming Pavilion, there is a six-piece Nanmu screen. The carving on the wood screen, rendered extremely intricate, is among the best decorations found in the Central Wu region (page 270). Regrettably, the pavilion faces west, and so damages to this screen caused by weather and the sun cannot be avoided.

The southwest corner of the east section is an area of new creation, arrayed with some featureless rockeries, which cannot be compared with the structure of the original garden.

West Section: The west section looks like what remained of the East Garden constructed durig the Ming dynasty. The hill is built by compacting earth and placing rocks at selected locations. This is just like the old technique summarized by Li Yu (李渔) as "small hill is built with rocks, while large hill with soil." As a result the large grove of maple trees growing on the hill receives sufficient nutrients from the earthen hill.

There are two pavilions situated within the maple grove. One is Shuxiao Ting (the Free Roaring Pavilion, 舒 啸 亭, page 274) which has

西部园林以时代而论，似为明东园旧规，山用积土，间列黄石，犹是李渔所云"小山用石，大山用土"的老办法，因此漫山枫树，得以滋根。林中配二亭：一为舒啸亭（274 页），系圆攒尖；一为至乐亭（272 页），六边形，系仿天平山范祠御碑亭而略变形的，在苏南还是创见。前者隐于枫林间，后者据西北山腰，可以上下眺望。南环清溪，植桃柳成荫，原期使人至此有世外之感，但有意为之，顿成做作，以人工胜天然在园林中实是不易的事。溪流终点，则为活泼泼地（250 页），一阁临水，水自阁下流入，人在阁中，仿佛跨溪之上，不觉有尽头了。唯该区假山，经数度增修，殊失原态。

北部旧构已毁，今新建，无亭台花木之胜。

a tapered cone shape roof. The other pavilion is the hexagonal shaped Zhile Ting (the Delightful Pavilion, 至乐亭, page 272). This pavilion is a transformation based on the Imperial Stela Pavilion (御碑亭) found at Fan's Ancestral Temple (范祠) at the Tianping Mountain (天平山). The Free Roaring Pavilion crouches amongst the maple trees. The Delightful Pavilion snuggles on the northwest slope of the hill. The two pavilions are within sight of each other.

The south side of the hill is surrounded by a clear creek flowing in the shade of peach and willow trees growing along the banks. The original purpose of these arrangements is to create an out of the world environment. But it seems too artificial to be real here. It is not easy to make a man-made scenery to outshine a natural one, especially in a garden.

At the end of the creek is Huopopodi (the Place of Liveliness, 活泼泼地, page 250). There is a pavilion built astride the water. The creek enters and submerges beneath the pavilion, which creates an illusion that the creek flows onwards. However, the rockeries in this area have lost most of their original outlook after various additions and repairs over the years.

North section: The original structures in the north section have all been destroyed. And the new buildings in this section do not have any outstanding features.

PART FOUR

The typical gardens in the region south of Yangtze are small in scale, but are adorned with picturesque sceneries of steep cliffs and deep gorges along clear streams and emerald pools. Qian Yong (钱　泳) said: "Building a garden is just like writing a poem. It must be structured according to the rules." The best garden should have such architectural elements as hills, ponds, pavilions, halls, and verandas in a way that offers ever refreshing, enchanting and kaleidoscopic scenes and that does not fall into any pre-existing norms. Therefore, in terms of planning and space design, it is highly desirable to make the landscape look more expansive, eye-catching and ever-changing. In genereal, overall garden planning in Suzhou can be grouped into several categories as described below.

Water as the theme of the garden: In this type of design a water body is located in the middle of a garden surrounded by halls and pavilions connected by verandas. Small bridges sit astride the water to provide easy access. In a large pond, it is advisable to put up some islets. These types of designs are found in gardens such as Wangshi Yuan (the Master-of-Nets Garden, 网 师 园) and the central part of Yiyuan (the Garden of Pleasance, 怡园). Changyuan at Miaotang Xiang (the Garden of Free Will, 庙堂巷畅园) is situated within a relatively constricted space. Its design is as delicate as that of a bonsai. A small body of water lies in the middle, surrounded by verandas and buildings. The theme of the Lingering Garden seems to be the water body in its center section. However, Master Liu Dunzhen (刘敦桢) believes that, when this garden is viewed in its entirety, its theme is actually the group of structures in

四

江南园林占地不广，然千岩万壑，清流碧潭，皆宛然如画，正如钱泳所说："造园如作诗文，必使曲折有法。"对于山水、亭台、厅堂、楼阁、曲池、方沼、花墙、游廊等之安排划分，必使风花雪月，光景常新，不落窠臼，始为上品。因此，对于总体布局及空间处理，务使有扩大之感，观之不尽，而风景多变，极尽规划之能事。总体布局可分以下几种。

中部以水为主题，贯以小桥，绕以游廊，间列亭台楼阁，大者中列岛屿，此类如网师园以及怡园等之中部。庙堂巷畅园，地颇狭小，一水居中，绕以廊屋，宛如盆景。留园虽以水为主，然刘师敦桢认为，该园以整体而论当以东部建筑群为主，这话亦有其理存在着。

以山石为全园之主题，因是区无水源可得，且无洼地可利用，故不能不以山石为主题使其突出，固设计中一法。如西百花巷程氏园无水可托，不得不如此。环秀山庄范围小，不能凿大池，亦以山石为主，略引水泉，俾山有生机，岩现活态，苔痕鲜润，草木华滋，宛然若真山水了。

基地积水弥漫，而占地尤广，布置遂较自由，不能为定法所囿。如拙政园、五亩园等较大者，更能发挥开朗变化的能事，尤其拙政园中部的一些小山大有张涟所云"平冈小坡，曲岸回沙"，都是运用人工方法来符合自然的境界。计成《园冶》云："虽由人作，宛自天开。"刘师敦桢主张："池水以聚为主，以分为辅。小园聚胜于分，大园虽可分，但须宾主分明。"网师园与拙政园是两个佳例，皆苏州园林上品。

前水后山，复构堂于水前，坐堂中穿水遥对山石，而堂则若水榭，横卧波面。文衙弄艺圃布局即如是，北寺塔东芳草园亦仿佛似之。

its east section. This opinion definitely deserves consideration.

Hills and rocks as the theme: This is an accepted practice when there is no readily available water source or low land within the garden. In such a case, it becomes a necessity to use hills and rocks as a theme to accentuate the landscape. Cheng's Garden in Xibaihua Xiang (西百花巷程氏园) is an example of such design. Huanxiu Shanzhuang (the Mountain Villa with Embracing Beauty, 环秀山庄) occupies a small land, where it is difficult to dig a large pond. As a consequence the designer picked hills and rocks as the theme, and introduced springs to make them come to life. Well-nourished, the moss turns green and the grass becomes lush. The whole landscape is an image of nature.

In case of designing a garden with an expansive water surface, there is a lot of flexibility. Usually, this type of gardens is relatively large. Its site planning should not be restricted by any hard and fast rules. For the large gardens such as the Humble Administrator's Garden and Wumu Yuan (the Five Acres Garden, 五亩园), wide vision and variability are the keys to site planning. For example, the hills in the center section of the Humble Administrator's Garden are transformed with human hand into nature-like scenery with "flat hilltop and smooth slopes along the curved sand shores", as described by Zhang Lian (张涟) in his essay. Ji Cheng (计成) wrote in *Yuanye* (*Craft of Gardens*, 《园冶》): "A garden should look as if created by nature though it is made through human efforts." Master Liu Dunzhen held that "water body in a garden should be concentrated, allowing only a small part diverted. In a small garden, concentration of water body is better than dispersed water system. In a large garden dispersing water body is viable but it should be done as a foil to the concentrated water area". Both the Humble Administrator's Garden and the Master-of-Nets Garden are exemplary designs of this type in Suzhou gardens.

Placement of a pond in front of Halls and with hills as background: In this deployment the halls are like waterside pavilions astride the waves. When sitting in the lounges, one enjoys a view of hills and rocks far across the pond. This type of layout is witnessed at Yipu in Wenya Long (the Garden of Cultivation, 文衙弄艺圃). The layout of FangcaoYuan (芳草园) on the east side of Beisi Ta (the North Temple Pagoda, 北寺塔) seems to have some resemblance to this type of design.

Placement of a pond and hills in the center surrounded by buildings and verandas: The array of buildings at different heights harmonize well with the hills and water in the center. This type of layout is rare in Suzhou. The only plausible example is the east side of Ouyuan at Xiaoxinqiao Xiang (the Couple's Garden Retreat, 小新桥巷耦园). The small garden of Han family on Dongbei Jie (东北街韩氏小园) bears some resemblance to this layout. But there are buildings only on two sides. As regard to Banyuan at Zhongyouji Xiang (中由吉巷半园) and Song family garden at Xiuxian Xiang (修仙巷宋氏园), the buildings cluster only on one side.

The Suzhou gardens built in the Ming dynasty closely resemble natural landscape. These design practices, as summarized by later architects such as Ji Cheng (计成) and Zhang Lian (张涟), took advantage of the original scenery and made

中列山水，四周环以楼及廊屋，高低错落，迤逦相续，与中部山石相呼应，如小新桥巷耦园东部，在苏州尚不多见。东北街韩氏小园，亦略取是法，不过楼屋仅有两面。中由吉巷半园、修仙巷宋氏园皆有一面用楼。

明代园林，接近自然，犹是计成、张涟辈后来所总结的办法，利用原有地形，略加整理，其所用石，在苏州大体以黄石为主，如拙政园中部二小山及绣绮亭亭下的。黄石虽无湖石玲珑剔透，然掇石有法，反觉浑成，既无矫揉做作之态，且无累石不固的危险。我们能从这种方法中细细探讨，在今日造园中还有不少优良传统可以吸收学习的。到清代造园皆以湖石叠砌，贪多好奇，每以湖石之多少与一峰之优劣与他园计较短长。试以怡园而论，购洞庭山三处废园之石累积而成，一峰一石，自有上选，但其西北部之一区，石骨外露，卒无活态，即其一例。可见"小山用石"，非全无寸土，不然树木将无所依托了。环秀山庄虽改建于乾隆间，数弓之地，深溪幽壑，势若天成，运用宋人山水的所谓"斧劈法"，再以镶嵌出之，简洁遒劲（298页），其水则迂回曲折，山石处处滋润，苍岩欣欣欲活了，诚为江南园林的杰构。于此方知设计者若非胸有丘壑，挥洒自如者焉能至斯？学养之功可见重要了。

掇山既须以原有地形为据，但自然之态，变化多端，无一定成法，可是自然的形成与发展，亦有一定的规律可循。"师古人不如师造化"，实有其理在。我们今日能通乎此理，从自然景物加以分析，证以古人作品，评其妍媸，撷其菁华，构成最美丽的典型。奈何苏州所见晚期园林，什九已成"程式化"，从不在整体考虑，每以亭、台、池、馆妄加拼凑，尤以掇山造石，皆举一峰片石，视之为古

only minor modifications as needed. The rocks used to pile up hills are primarily Huangshi (yellow rocks，黄石), as found in the two smal hills as well as the mound under the Paeonia Suffruticosa Pavilion in the center section of the Humble Administrator's Garden. Although yellow rocks are not as exquisite as Hushi (lake stones，湖石) in shape, the hills piled with yellow rocks look just as natural if done properly, without any affected air and any risk of collapse. Many fresh ideas and techniques may be discovered from studying these traditional designs in detail and hence can be applicable to today's garden construction.

During the Qing dynasty, the use of lake stones in rockery design became popular. So much so that there emerged a trend of coveting more rockeries and seeking the novelty of their structure. The number of rockeries and the quality of a single rockery thus became the sole criterion in evaluating the superiority of a garden. A typical example is the construction of the Garden of Pleasance, for which the best lake rocks from three garden ruins in Dongting Mountain area were used. However, in its northwest section, the stone skeletons of the rockeries were exposed and hence lacked any greenery and life. What's more, the statement of "small hills are made out of rocks" does not mean no use of soil at all in hill construction. Without soil, trees and plants will not be able to subsist. On the other hand, though renovated extensively in Qianlong period of the Qing dynasty, the Mountain Villa with Embracing Beauty is considered as one of the best gardens in the region south of Yangtze for its superb rockery arrangement. In a small piece of land, probably within a stone's throw, the mini-landscape of creek running quietly among secluded deep gorges seems to be a natural wonder. In the Song dynasty, a painting technique called "chopping with axe" (斧 劈 法) was developed in painting rocks and hills. This painting style was adopted in the rockery design of the Mountain Villa with Embracing Beauty, which strikes one with its boldness and force (page 298). With winding waterway nurturing the hillsides and rocks, the cliffs come alive with joyful green. Such an artistic perfection in design cannot be achieved if one has neither life experience nor an ability to put his knowledge into play with facility and dexterity. Here one can see the importance of conscientious study and self-cultivation.

Arrangement of a hill in garden design should be based on the topography of an existing terrain. The natural topography is variable, which makes it impossible to follow a fixed format or pattern in arranging hills in a garden. However, any formation and development in nature has its own law to abide by. Therefore, the saying "learning form Creator is more worthwhile than learning from ancients" has a grain of truth. Only by thoroughly understanding this philosophy, can one consummate a good design in garden rockery. In brief, one should initiate the design with a careful analysis of existing landscape. In regards to the previous work done by the ancients, one needs to understand its essence of beauty and try to apply it to today's work. At same time, one should also try to avoid replicating the awkward design done in the past. Unfortunately, this philosophy was not very well followed in Suzhou gardens constructed lately. The majority of these designs were just a jumble of buildings and ponds pieced together without any careful study. A large number of designers fell into the mindset of going by a fixed formula without any iota of innovation.

This is especially true of the arranging of hills and stacking of rocks. Instead of taking the whole landscape into consideration, these poeple just treat each piece of rock as an antique and rigged up these rocks together without a careful planning of their contrast with plants and their harmony with buildings. As mentioned earlier, the Garden of Pleasance was intended to benefit from the best designs of all the gardens in Suzhou. But the end product is a mere patchwork of structures, which does not signify a success. This is a lesson to today's garden architects.

As to the water in a garden, what is of necessity is to locate a source. A pond without a source is destined to become stagnant. For example, pre-existing lakes and swamps are used to create water surface in the Humble Administrator's Garden. A source of water is found in the Mountain Villa with Embracing Beauty by digging up an underground spring. The spring water is limited in volume but fresh and limpid enough to nurture the plants.

Proper design methods should be applied to create the impression of expansiveness of water surface in spite of a limited garden space. In general, there are two common practices to achieve this effect. The first method is to take advantage of an irregular water surface and sprinkle it with some islets. The islets are all connected via small bridges. With this arrangement, the space over the water is not plainly visible at a glance. The second method is to design with meticulous care of shoreline and upstream sources. The design involves placing various small bays or fjords along the shoreline, which bring about an impression that the water flows from a variety of sources with neither beginning nor ending. It adds

董，对于花树的衬托，建筑物的调和等，则有所忽略，这是今日园林设计者要引以为鉴的。如怡园欲集诸园之长，但全局涣散，似未见成功。

园林之水，首在寻源，因无源之水必死水。如拙政园利用原来池沼；环秀山庄掘地得泉，水虽涓涓，亦必清冽可爱。但园林面积既小，欲使有汪洋之概，则在设计时的运用，其法有二：其一池面利用不规则的平面，间列岛屿，上贯以小桥，在空间上使人望去，不觉一览无余。其二留心曲岸水口的设计，故意做成许多湾头，望之仿佛有许多源流，如是则水来去无尽头，有深壑藏幽之感。至于曲岸水口之利用芦苇，杂以菰蒲，则更显得隐约迷离，这是以较大的园林应用才妙。留园活泼泼地，水榭临流，溪至榭下已尽，但必流入一部分，则俯视之下，榭若跨溪上，水不觉终止。南显子巷惠荫园水假山，系层叠巧石如洞曲，引水灌之，点以步石，人行

a sensation of seclusion by hiding the sources in deep gorges. This effect of illusion is further enhanced by planting reed and wild rice at the upstream sources. However, the latter method is viable for larger gardens.

The building Huopopodi (the Place of Liveliness, 活泼泼地) in the Lingering Garden is a waterside pavilion located at the end of a creek. But a part of water still flows underneath the building. With such an arrangement, the pavilion seems to stand over a never ending creek. The water rockery in Huiyin Yuan at Nanxianzi Xiang (南显子巷惠荫园) is made from layers of carefully stacked rocks. Water is siphoned into the tunnels formed within the rockery. While pacing upon the stepping stones propped up in the water, one feels like walking along deep gorges. And a hut is placed on the top of the cave. This unique structure found in central Wu region is based on the design of Zhaoyiwang's garden in the Southern Song dynasty (南宋杭州赵翼王园). The highlight of the Garden of Canglang Ting (the Canglang Pavilion, 沧浪亭) is its rockery. There is a waterside veranda on its west side. This veranda rises in elevation so drastically as to offer a bird's eye view of the pond deep below. It is unfortunate the design does not fully achieve the dramatec effect because there is no flowing water in the pond. This type of detail should not be neglected in design in order to achieve consummate effect.

As will be discussed in detail later, bridges in Suzhou gardens are typically close to the water surface. The bridges in the Garden of Cultivation are almost level with the water (page 296), which sets off the height and steepness of the rocks on the shore. Although the bridges in the Garden of Pleasance are a little bit away from the water, they are sufficiently lower than the surrounding rockeries, which is still acceptable. What would the contrast be when building a bridge over a small creek? It is not hard to imagine why our ancients used stepping stones instead of a bridge. This method seems more in keeping with natural order. There are few examples of waterfall in Suzhou gardens. The waterfall over the building eave found in the Mountain Villa with Embracing Beauty is an exception.

Building structures such as halls, towers, pavilions, kiosks and terraces compose other major elements beside water ponds, creeks, rockeries and hills in Chinese gardens. Gardens in the region south of Yangtze are famed for their tranquility and elegance. The style of builiding structures in these gardens should be exquisite and in harmony with the surroundings. So their position, terrain and exterior appearace should be taken into consideration. The famous book of Chinese garden construction, *Yuanye* (*Craft of Gardens*, 《园冶》), stated: "At the strart of a garden construction, one needs to decide how the hall should be built. The building should match the scene. Facing south is preferred. It is also desirable to plant some trees in the courtyard." This is the principle followed in the construction of the gardens south of Jiangsu, such as the Hall of Distant Fragrance in the Humble Administrator's Garden and the Hanbi Mountain Villa in the Lingering Garden.

As to the positioning of a hall in a garden, there is no strictly defined principles to go by, though some guidelines and advice can be found in several classic books of Chinese garden construction, such as *Yuanye*, *Changwu Zhi* (*Treatise on Superfluous Things*, 《长物

其间，如入洞壑，洞上则构屋。此种形式为吴中别具一格者，殆系南宋杭州赵翼王园中之遗制。沧浪亭以山为主，但西部的步碕廊突然逐渐加高，高瞰水潭，自然临渊莫测，惜是潭平时无涓涓活流，致设计者事与愿违，斯亦不能不注意的。艺圃的桥与水几平（296页），反之两岸山石愈显高峻了。怡园之桥虽低于山，但与水尚有一些距离，还不失为有所依据的。至于小溪作桥，在对比之下其情况何如？不难想象。古人遂改用"点其步石"的方法，则更为自然有致了。瀑布除环秀山庄檐瀑外，他则罕有。

中国园林除水、石、池、沼外，建筑物如厅、堂、斋、台、亭、榭、轩、卷、廊等，都是构成园林的主要部分，然江南园林以幽静雅淡为主，故建筑物务求轻巧，方始相称，所以在建筑物的地点、平面以及外观上不能不注意。《园冶》云："凡园圃立基，定厅堂为主，先取乎景，妙在朝南，倘

有乔木数株，仅就中庭一二。"苏南园林尚守是法，如拙政园远香堂，留园涵碧山房等皆是。至于楼台亭阁的地位，虽无成法，但"按基形式"，"格式随宜"，"随方制象，各有所宜"，"一榱一桷，必令出自己裁"，"花间隐榭，水际安亭"，还是在设计人从整体出发而加以灵活应用。古代如《园冶》《长物志》《工段营造录》等，虽有述及，最后亦指出我们不能守为成法的。试以拙政园而论，我们自高处俯视，建筑物虽然是随宜安排的，其方向差不多都依地形而改变，其外观给人的感觉是轻快为主。平面正方形、长方形、多边形、圆形等皆有。屋顶形式则有歇山、单面歇山、硬山、悬山、攒尖等，而无庑殿式。即使歇山、硬山、悬山，亦多数采用卷棚式。其翼角起翘类多用"水戗发戗"的办法，因此翼角起翘低而外观轻快。檐下玲珑的挂落、柱间微弯的吴王靠，得能

志 》）, *Gongduan Yingzao Lu* (*Notes of Hall Construction*, 《工段营造录》). The following are some guidelines quoted from these books. "Form of a building accords with the base on which it is built." "Arrangement of a building should be consistent with its surrounding." "Each aspect of the design should be considered separately to meet its own need." "Each corner is wrought according to its own feature." "A bower should be hidden in a grove. A kiosk should be positioned by water." In summary, one should not fall into a rut in designing a hall. Instead, one should proceed from the construction of a garden in its entirety and use some common sense in hall design.

Take the Humble Administrator's Garden as an example. If we take an aerial view of the garden, we can find that its buildings mix themselves harmoniously with the changing landscape. Their exterior look is elegant and sprightly, no matter what plane views are presented, rectangular, square, polygon, or cicle. There is also a rich variety of roof styles, including the gable roof with either flushing purlins （硬山）or outstanding purlins （悬山）, or the gable-on-hip roof either on both gable sides （歇山）or on single gable side （单面歇山）, or the pyramid-like pointed shape roof （攒尖）. The only exception is the palace-like hip roof, that is to say, a hip roof with a heavy eave structure and a heavy outstanding ridge （庑 殿 式）. Most roofs in the garden are without the main ridge, making a smooth curving transition at its top line （卷棚式）. The upturned corner eave adopts a "water spraying" style （水戗发戗）, which starts the upturning at a low angle and thus looks light. This light touch of corner eave is in line with the intricate decorative border beneath the eaves, as well as the balustrade called Wuangkao (Backrest for King Wu，吴王靠）slightly curved between the building pillars.

Regarding the elevated structure of buildings, the center section of the Lingering Garden is a good example. Looking eastward from the Osmanthus Fragrance Pavilion, the Winding Stream Tower comes in view with its gable-on-hip roof. Its ground floor is designed like a foundation of a platform, with architrave in parallel to the water and separated from the upper floor. With such an arrangement, this two stages tower does not look overwhelming in height. The locations of the three buildings, namely, the Winding Stream Tower, the Western Tower, and the Refreshing Breeze Pavilion by the Lake, hold off from each other. The roof structures of these three buildings are of the same type but each is slightly distinctive in its own way. Such arrangement matches well with the rockeries and water around them. A contrast of virtual and real visions of architrave and wall is created through the arrangement of brick framed tracery windows casting sparse and light flowery patterns. This is a unique feature found in Suzhou gardens. In particular, with the reflection of all these structures in the water the beauty of the scenery beggars any description. Set off by such a milieu, an aged tree leaning lonely over water seems more sturdy and vigorous.

Another prototype of flexible hall design is witnessed in the Hanbi Mountain Villa and the Pellucid Tower in the Lingering Garden. These two buildings are attached to each other. The roof structure of the Villa is a gable roof with flushing purlins on both sides. The roof structure of the Tower is a hybrid one, a simple gable with flushing perlins on the side attached to the Villa and a gable-on-hip structure on the open side. Usually, this special hybrid roof design would have looked odd when applied to a single independent buiding. Nevertheless, when applied in this particular case, the two adjacent buildings look more lively instead (page 205). A similar example is Changyuan (the Garden of Free Will, 畅园). This garden is narrow in width. With a pond in the middle, there is little space to build a pavilion. Consequently, a single side gable-on-hip structure is used in the place of waterside pavilion.

On the other hand, there are some cases in which the building desingn needs to be reconsidered. One example is the pavilion at the corner of the east section of the Lingering Garden. A hexagonal pyramid roof structure is used in this case. In order to seek a visually delicate and graceful effect, a "water spraying" style is adopted on its upturning corner eaves. However, the pillars are too thin and too tall to support such a roof structure. Consequently, this pavilion looks out of proportion. The Free Roaring Pavilion and the Delightful Pavilion are both located in the west section of the Lingering Garden. These two pavilions both suffer form disproportions. The Free Roaring Pavilion is small but not delicate. The roof of the Delightful Pavilion seems too heavy though full of variation. Indeed, this is a common problem in recent pavilion construction in Suzhou region. The modern time artisans of Xiangshan generation preferred pavilion structure with overly high roof and thin columns. The exterior look of these pavilions is not necessarily attractive. This modern design is divergent from the Ming style design found in Yipu (the Garden of Cultivation, 艺圃), which has a slightly lower roof structure to enhance the stability of a building.

取得一致。建筑物在立面的处理，以留园中部而论，我们自闻木樨香轩东望，对景主要建筑物是曲溪楼，用歇山顶，其外观在第一层做成仿佛台基的形状，与水相平行的线脚与上层分界，虽系二层看去不觉其高耸了。而尤其曲溪楼、西楼、清风池馆三者的位置各有前后，屋顶立面皆同中寓不同，与下部的立峰水石都很相称。古木一树斜横波上，益增苍古，而墙上的砖框、漏窗，上层的窗棂与墙面虚实的对比，疏淡的花影，都是苏州园林特有的手法，尤其倒映水中，其景更美。明瑟楼与涵碧山房相邻，前者为卷棚歇山，后者为卷棚硬山，然两者相联，不能不用变通的办法。明瑟楼歇山山面仅作一面，另一面用垂脊，不但不觉得其难看，反觉生动有变化（205页）。他如畅园，因基地较狭长，中又系水池，水榭无法安排，卒用单面歇山，实系同出一法。反之，东园一角亭，为求轻巧起见，六角攒尖顶

In the last analysis, any single buiding design should be conceived in light of the whole garden arrangement. As to plane variability the design calls for a fluent and smooth flow in a winding pathway as well as a feeling of spaciousness in a densely furnished hall. The size of a building is completely dependant on its need and milieu. It can be as small as one bay or two bays, some times even two and half bays. The Malus Spectabilis Garden Court in the Humble Administrator's Garden is only a two bays court, with the major bay obviously wider than the other. The Worshipping Stone Pavilion in the Lingering Garden is two and half bays wide, among which the half bay is the most intriguing. Only up to this point one can really appreciate the design principles presented in the classic book *Yuanye* (*Craft of Gardens*, 《园冶》). High and low in profiling, left and right in balancing, virtual and real in contrasting, every aspect is not to be ignored in designing a garden building.

The furnishing and decoration of the following places are among the best in Suzhou gardens. They are Wangshi Yuan (the Master-of-Nets Garden, 网师园), the Flower Hall in Gu's House at Tieping Xiang (铁瓶巷顾宅花厅), Cheng's Garden in Xibaihua Xiang (西百花巷程氏园), the Flower Hall in Wu's House in Dashitou Xiang (大石头巷吴宅花厅), the east and west Flower Halls in Ren's House in Tieping Xiang (铁瓶巷任宅东西花厅), as well as Wan's Garden in Wangxianma Xiang (王洗马巷万氏园). For additional details on this subject please refer to another book of mine, *Collection of Decorative Devices*. In particular, Wan's Garden in Wangxianma Xiang is a small garden but its study is well isolated from the rest of the garden, creating a uniquely secluded environment. In regards to some other gardens, there is much room for improvement in their furnishing and decoration. The Lingering Garden is overly complex. It looks coarse and crude with few exquisite designs in between. In the Humble Administrator's Garden, although some fine decorations can be found, most are plain and invariant. This is the result of piecing together only what are available during the restoration and repairs. As far as Yiyuan (the Garden of Pleasure, 怡园) is concerned, almost all original furnishings have been lost, except the Boat-Like Pavilion, which is among the best in the central Wu region (page 312).

Verandas are the veins and arteries of a garden. They deserve special attention due to their importance. Double-corridor verandas are quite common in today's Suzhou gardens. This is kind of veranda with a wall in the middle separating the veranda into two sides. Tracery windows (see my writing *On Tracery Windows* for additional details) are built in this center wall. The two sides of the veranda are available for passage and often referred to as inner or outer corridor respectively. The double-corridor veranda is used mostly as the boundary of an open style garden, such as the one along the water in the Garden of Canglang Ting (the Canglang Pavilion , 沧浪亭 , page 347). It is used also inside a garden as a division in order to increase an illusion of spaciousness or as a transition between the entry and the garden interior. One such example is the double-corridor veranda found in the Garden of Pleasance (page 305). Other than the function mentioned aboved, this double -corridor also provides a shade to Suihan Caolu (the Evergreen Thatched Cottage, 岁

的翼角用"水戗发戗",其上部又太重,柱身瘦而高,在整个比例上顿觉不稳。西部舒啸亭、至乐亭,前者小而不见玲珑,后者屋顶虽多变化,亦觉过重,都是比例上的缺陷。苏南筑亭,晚近香山匠师每将屋顶提得过高,但柱身又细,整个外观未必真美。反视艺圃明代遗构,屋顶略低,较平稳得多。总之,单体建筑必然要考虑到与全园的整体关系才是。至于平面变化,虽洞房曲户,亦必做到曲处有通,实处有疏。小型轩馆,一间、二间,或二间半均可,皆视基地,随宜安排。如拙政园海棠春坞面阔二间,一大一小,宾主分明。留园揖峰轩面阔二间半,而尤妙于半间,方信《园冶》所云有所独见之处。建筑物的高下得势,左右呼应,虚实对比,在在都须留意。王洗马巷万氏园(原为任氏),园虽小,书房部分自成一区,极为幽静。其装修与铁瓶巷任宅东西花厅、顾宅花厅、网师园、西百花巷程氏园、大石头巷

吴宅花厅等（详见拙著《装修集录》）都是苏州园林中之上选。至于他园尚多商量处，如留园太繁琐伧俗，佳者甚少；拙政园精者固有，但多数又觉简单无变化，力求一律，皆修理中东拼西凑或因陋就简所造成。怡园旧装修几不存，而旱船为吴中之尤者（312页），所遗装修极精。

园林游廊为园林的脉络，在园林建筑中处极重的地位，故特地说明一下。今日苏州园林廊之常见者为复廊，即廊系两面游廊，中隔以粉墙，间以漏窗（详见拙编《漏窗》），使墙内外皆可行走。此种廊大都用于不封闭性的园林，如沧浪亭的沿河（347页）。或一园中须加以间隔，欲使空间扩大，并使入门有所过渡，如怡园的复廊便是一例，此廊显然是仿前者。它除此作用外，因岁寒草庐与拜石轩之间不为西向的阳光与朔风所直射，用以阻之，而阳光通过漏窗，其图案更觉玲珑剔透（305页）。游廊有陆上、

寒草庐）and Baishi Xuan (the Rock Worshipping Pavilion, 拜石轩). It protects the two buildings from the afternoon sunshine and the strong west wind. On the other hand, the sunlight sieving through the tracery windows of the partition wall makes a fantastic view of intricate lattice patterns.

In general, verandas can be classified according to their location into those on land and those by water. It is also possible to categorize verandas in terms of their shape into winding verandas and straight verandas. The shape of a veranda should avoid being flat and straight. On the other hand, the verandas in present day Suzhou gardens are overly windy by design. This type of designs lacks a natural touch and looks stilted. An example of such design is the passage along the north wall of the central section in the Lingering Garden. This veranda is accosted by a bricks balustrade, which seems stifling and does not match the decorative border at the top. The placement of columns between stone tablets further adds oppressiveness to the design. A better design is achieved by using hollow bricks for the waterside verandas found in both Ren's House in Tieping Xiang (铁瓶巷任宅) and the west side of the Humble Administraror's Garden. For the veranda "A Winding Way in Willow Shades" in the Humble Administor's Garden, wood balustrade is used on the waterfront side, while Wuwangkao (Backrest for King Wu, 吴王靠 , a bench style balustrade with straight upward backrest) is placed on the opposite side. This type of veranda design stands to reason (page 148).

The best waterside veranda can be found in the west side of the Humble Administrator's Garden (page 156). There is not only an extremely well designed zigag passage, but also slight slope. This is just like what is called "floating veranda takes you across the water" in *Yuanye* (*Craft of Gardens*, 《园冶》). The planting of plantain or the setup of a lake stone rockery along selected winding areas of the veranda with small waterside pavilions standing by are some of the highlights in this design (page 157-158).

Ascending verandas can be found along border walls of various Suzhou gardens. This type of veranda is used sparingly in gardens such as Shizilin (the Lion Forest Garden, 狮子林), the Lingering Garden, and the Humble Administrator's Garden. It is important to pay attention to the relationship of the veranda's slope with the hill's height. Otherwise, an improperly designed ascending veranda would be top heavy and out of balance. If the space available is limited or uneven in width, it is advisable to use either a single side slope, or combination of single side and two sides slope as needed. This type of design can be found in the west part of the Lingering Garden. The planting of bamboo or plantain, and placement of lake stones along the inside corners of a winding veranda will always result in a spot of wonderful scenery.

Li Dou (李斗) wrote: "A wooden structure along with brick walls makes a passage. When the passage is curved along a land slope it becomes a touring passage. If the passage is both curved and bended along its way, it is turned into a winding veranda. When curvature is removed, it makes for an addressed pathway. If two ways run opposite to each other, it is called a paired way. Those for the purpose of passage are walkways. If for wandering, it is named stepping way. When

水上之分，又有曲廊、直廊之别，但忌平直生硬。今日苏州诸园所见，过分求曲，则反觉生硬勉强，如留园中部北墙下的。至其下施以砖砌栏杆，一无空虚之感，与上部挂落不称，柱夹砖中，僵直滞重。铁瓶巷任宅及拙政园西部水廊小榭，易以镂空之砖，似此较胜。拙政园旧时柳荫路曲，临水一面栏杆用木制，另一面上安吴王靠，是有道理的（148 页）。水廊佳者，如拙政园西部的，不但有极佳的曲折，并有适当的坡度，诚如《园冶》所云的"浮廊可渡"，允称佳构（156页）。尤其可取的就是曲处置湖石芭蕉（157—158 页），配以小榭，更觉有变化。爬山游廊在苏州园林中狮子林、留园、拙政园略点缀一二，大都是用于园林边墙部分。设计此种廊时应注意到坡度与山的高度问题，否则运用不当，顿成头重脚轻，上下不协调。在地形狭宽不同的情况下，可运用一面坡的，或一面坡与二面坡并用，如留园西部的。曲廊的曲处是留虚的好办法，随便点缀一些竹石、芭蕉，都是极妙的小景。李斗云："板上甃砖谓之响廊，随势曲折谓之游廊，愈折愈曲谓之曲廊，不曲者修廊，相向者对廊，通往来者走廊，容徘徊者步廊，入竹为竹廊，近水为水廊。花间偶出数尖，池北时来一角，或依悬崖，故作危槛，或跨红板，下可通舟，递迢于楼台亭榭之间，而轻好过之。廊贵有栏。廊之有栏，如美人服半臂，腰为之细，其上置板为飞来椅，亦名美人靠，其中广者为轩。"言之尤详，可资参考。今日复有廊外植芭蕉呼为"蕉廊"，植柳呼为"柳廊"。夏日人行其间，更觉翠色侵衣，溽暑全消；冬日则阳光射入，温和可喜，用意至善。而古时以廊悬画称"画廊"，今日壁间嵌诗条石，都是极好的应用。

园林中水面之有桥，正如陆路之有廊，重要可知，苏州园林习见之桥，一种为梁式石桥，可分直桥、九曲桥、五曲桥、三曲桥、弧形桥等，

leading to a bamboo grove, it is designated as a bamboo path. When built by the water it is addressed as a waterside veranda. At some places it sits against cliff, with high rail. At other places it stands over the water, with boats flowing beneath. Here and there, it looms in the flower grove. Now and then, it emerges at the shore. At most places it winds among pavilions, towers, and halls, providing an easy passage. A veranda cannot miss its rail. A veranda with a nice rail is just like a beauty wearing a pretty short sleeve which gives prominence to her slender waist. Putting boards over the rail makes a flying-in bench, or what is called Meirenkao (Backrest for Beauty, 美人靠). The portion of a veranda with wide interior space is called Xuan (轩 , a veranda type hall)." Li Dou's writing provides a detailed overview of verandas and serves as a good reference. Nowadays some applications of garden veranda have been found. For example, the veranda lined on both sides with plantain is called a Jiaolang (Plantain-thronged Veranda), while a veranda ringed with willow trees is called a Liulang (Willow-sheltered Veranda). These verandas offer verdant shade to keep the passage cool during summer while in winter are bathed in warm sunshine. During ancient times, some verandas were used as a gallery to exhibit paintings. In recent years, some of these verandas are decorated with inlaid stone tablets inscribed with poems on the surface. All these are superb adaptations of ancient verandas.

Bridge is an integral part of a garden. In a garden, a bridge to the water is as significant as a veranda to the road. Clapper bridge is the most common bridge found in Suzhou gardens. This type of bridges can be categorized into several styles including straight bridge, zigzag bridge with three, five or nine bends, and arc shaped bridge. The height of the bridge can be either level with the shore, as found in more recent designs, or lower than the shore and slightly elevated from the water, as found in the older bridges. The bridges following older design are still available in the Garden of Cultivation, Jichang Yuan of Wuxi (Garden for Lodging One's Expansive Feelings, 无锡寄畅园, page 355).), and various gardens in Changshu The bridges found in the Garden of Pleasance as well as in the ruins of Yan family garden in Mudu also bear resemblance to this design, but they are slightly higher in elevation from the water surface. In my view, the older design is motivated to achieve the following effects. Above all, walking through a bridge at water level gives people a feeling of treading the water. It enhances the perception of vastness of the water and of precariousness of the bridge. Secondly, a lower bridge surface will form a sharp contrast with the height of the surrounding buildings and hills. The steepeness of cliffs and buildings seem more impressive. The bridge in the Garden for Lodging One's Expansive Feelings is arranged in a secluded canyon beneath a plateau. Behind the plateau is the transferred scene of Huishan Mountain in distance. This arrangement demonstrates the complexity of garden design techniques employed during the Ming dynasty.

On the other hand, clapper bridges are often not deployed very carefully in today's gardens. They are designed without consideration of the surrounding landscape and the size of the bridge. In particular, the balustrade design is incompatible with both the bridge and surrounding environment

其位置有高于水面与岸相平的，有低于两岸浮于水面的。以时代而论，后者似较旧，我们今日在艺圃及无锡寄畅园（355页）、常熟诸园所见的都是如此，怡园及已毁木渎严家花园的亦仿佛似之，不过略高于水面一点。旧时为什么如此设计呢？它所表现的效果有二：第一，桥与水平，则游者凌波而过，水益显汪洋，桥更觉其危了。第二，桥低则山石建筑愈形高峻，与丘壑楼台自然成强烈对比。无锡寄畅园假山用平岗，其后以惠山为借景，岗下幽谷间施以是式桥，诚能发挥明代园林设计之高度技术。今日梁式桥往往不照顾地形，不考虑本身大小，随便安置，实属非当。而尤其栏杆高度、形式，都从不结合全桥及环境作一番研究，甚至于半封建半殖民地的铁栏杆都加了上去，如拙政园西部的。而上选者，如艺圃小桥、拙政园倚虹桥（93页）都是。拙政园中部的三曲五曲之桥，栏杆比例都还好，可惜桥本身略高一些，待霜亭与雪香云蔚亭二小山之间石桥，仅搁一石板，不施栏杆，极尽自然质朴之意，亦佳构（110页）。另一种为小型环洞桥，狮子林、网师园都有，以此二桥而论，前者不及后者为佳，因环洞桥不适宜建于水中部，水面既小，用此中阻，遂显庞大质实，略无空灵之感。后者建于东部水尽头，桥本身又小（300页），从西东望，辽阔的水面中倒影玲珑。反之，自桥西望，月门倒映水中，用意相同。中由吉巷半园，因地位狭小，将环洞变形，亦系出权宜之计。至于小溪，《园冶》所云"点其步石"的办法，尤能与自然相契合，实远胜架桥其上，可是此法今日差不多已成绝响了。

园林的路，《清闲供》云："门内有径，径欲曲"，"室旁有路，路欲分"。今日我们在苏州园林所见，还能如此。拙政园中部道路犹守明时旧规，从原来地形出发，加以变化，主次分明，曲折有度。环秀山庄面积小，不能不略作纤盘，但亦能恰到好

in terms of its height and style. In some designs, there are even wrought iron balustrades typically found in semi-feudal and semi-colonial times. The bridge in the west section of the Humble Administrator's Garden is such an example.

Regarding some good bridge designs, the small bridges in the Garden of Cultivation and the Leaning Against Rainbow Bridge in the Humble Administrator's Garden (page 93) are among the most admirable. The height of balustrade for the two zigzag bridges in the center section of the Humble Administrator's Garden is also appropriate. However, both bridges are slightly too elevated from the water surface. There is a stone bridge connecting the two islets where the Orange Pavilion and the Snow-Like Fragrant Prunus Mume Pavilion are located respectively. This bridge is made of only one single stone slab without any balustrades (page 110). This is a primitive but praise-worthy bridge design.

The other style of stone bridges in Suzhou gardens is the small stone arch bridge. They can be found in both the Lion Forest Garden and the Master-of-Nets Garden, but the former is not as good as the latter in design. The reason is obvious. In general, the water surface in Suzhou gardens is not very large. Arc bridge usually has a giant and solid body. Placing such a bridge across a small pond makes the view rather oppressive. In the Master-of-Nets Garden, this problem has been solved successfully. The bridge body there is quite small. It is built at the end of the water (page 300). When viewed from the west, an exquisite reflection of the bridge is clearly visible in the expansive water. And conversely, when looked from the east of the bridge, a moon gate is mirrored in the water.

The effect of these two arrangements is similar. In Banyuan at Zhongyouji Xiang (中由吉巷半园), the arc under the bridge is deformed to adapt to the available limited space. As regarding the way across a creek, the book *Yuanye* (*Craft of Gardens*, 《园冶》) said that "laying small stepping stones" is a more natural and much better approach than building a bridge. It is unfortunate this style of design is almost lost today.

The road in a garden is noted in the monograph *Qingxiangong* (*Provision of Leisure*, 《清闲供》) as "the trail inside a gate must be winding" and "the way beside a house must be extendable to all directions". For example, the trails in the center section of the Humble Administrator's Garden follow the original Ming dynasty architectural arrangement. They are winding in a graceful fashion along the land-shaped profile. There is a clear distinction between primary and auxiliary roads. The trais in the Mountain Villa with Embracing Beauty are more curvy and winding due to the limited space of the garden. But they are arranged properly and intriguingly. On the other hand, the trails in the Lion Forest Garden and the Garden of Pleasance are interlaced with each other in a way that is both unnatural and inexplicable. Indeed, any cutesy arrangement in the garden far removed from the nature is not truly artistic and should be avoided.

The pavement is another important aspect in the design of a garden. The pavements of a court front, a trail, or a main road are equally important and need to be considered carefully. In today's Suzhou gardens, bricks are commonly used to pave the main road. Its paving is relatively simple, and easy to form various patterns. Gravel pavements

处，行者有引人入胜之慨。然狮子林、怡园的（路），故作曲折，使人莫之所从，既悖自然之理，又多不近人情。因此，矫揉做作，与自然相距太远的安排，实在是不艺术的事。

铺地，在园林亦是一件重要的工作，不论庭前、曲径、主路，皆须极慎重考虑。今日苏州园林所见：有仄砖铺地，大都铺于主路，施工简单，拼凑图案自由。碎石地，用碎石仄铺，可用于主路、小径、庭前，上面间有用缸片点缀一些图案。或缸片仄铺间以瓷片的，用法同前。鹅子地，或鹅子间加瓷片拼凑成各种图案，视上述的要细致雅洁得多，但其缺点是石隙间的泥土，每为雨水及人力所冲扫而逐渐减少，又复较易长小草，保养费事，是需要改进的。冰裂地则用于庭前，苏南的做法有二：其一即冰纹石块平置地面，如拙政园远香堂前的（191 页），颇饶自然之趣，然亦有不平稳的流弊。其二则水纹石间交接处皆对卯拼成，施工难而坚固，如留园涵碧山房前（309 页）、铁瓶巷顾宅花厅的（325 页），都是极工整。至于庭前踏跺用天然石垒，如拙政园远香堂（191 页）及留园五峰仙馆前的（230 页），皆饶野趣。

　　园林的墙，有乱石墙、磨砖墙、漏砖墙、白粉墙等数种，苏州今日所见以白粉墙为最多。外墙有上开瓦花窗（漏窗开在墙顶部）的，内墙间开漏窗及砖框的，即所谓"粉墙花影"，为人乐道。磨砖墙，园内仅建筑物上酌用之。园门十之八九贴以水磨砖拼成的图案，如拙政园大门（72 页）。乱石墙只见于裙肩处。在上海南市薛家浜路旧宅中我曾见到冰裂纹上缀以梅花的，极精，似系明代旧物。西园以水漏窗花墙界定水面，亦别具一格（337 页）。

　　联对匾额在中国园林中正是如人之有须眉，是不能少的一件重要点缀品。苏州为人文荟萃之区，当时园林建造复有文人画家的参与，从人工上

can be used on either road or courtyard ground. It is usually speckled with clay or porcelain discs to form patterns. The pavements made of cobblestone, or cobblestone with porcelain discs are more elaborate and elegant than the pavements using brick or gravel. But they call for more maintenance. The earth filled between cobblesstones gets lost after rain wash or road sweeping and hence needs to be refilled regularly. Weeds growing in the earth also need to be removed periodically.

　　Ice cracking pavement is a special technique featuring the courtyard ground. Two kinds of this pavement are applied in the region south of Jiangsu. The first kind is just to place natural rocks on the ground leaving ice cracking veins around them, such as the pavement in front of the Hall of Distant Fragrance in the Humble Administrator's Garden (page 191). It looks natural, but has a difficulty to make the pavement evenly spaced. Another kind is to cut the rocks into slabs and then to match up these irregular slabs while paving, leaving crevices between them, such as the pavements in front of Hanbi Mountain Villa in the Lingering Garden (page 309) and Huating (the Flower Hall) in Gu's House at Tieping Xiang (page 325). This is a very difficult paving job. But it gives a solid and neat ground surface. Another related structure is the steps in front of a hall. Piling natural stones to form the steps creates an air of wilderness. A case in point is the kind of steps in front of the Hall of Distant Fragrance in the Humble Administrator's Garden (page 191) and the Celestial Hall of Five Peaks of the Lingering Garden (page 230).

Various kinds of walls are erected in Chinese gardens, such as gravel wall, water-milled brick wall, latticed brick wall, and stucco wall. Among them stucco wall is the most common in today's Suzhou gardens. Sometimes, tiles are put on top of outer wall to form a latticed top portion. In most cases inner walls are inlaid with brick-framed windows or tracery windows. This is commonly referred to as "flowery patterns on white-washed wall". The application of water-milled wall is limited to building structure. Most entrance gate wall is built by laying water-milled bricks in various patterns. A good example is the gate wall of the Humble Administrator's Garden (page 72). A wall can be divided into upper and lower parts. The lower part is called wall shirt. A short portion just above the wall skirt is called skirt shoulder. In Chinese gardens, gravel wall is mostly found at this portion of the wall. In an ancient house in Shanghai, I saw a very refined wall with ice cracking pattern dotted with plum flower, which is believed to be from the Ming dynasty. In the West Garden (戒幢律寺西园), a latticed window wall is built across water, a unique device indeed (page 337).

Antithetical couplet and horizontal tablet are important and necessary decorative elements in Chinese gardens. Their role is just like what the beard and the eyebrows play for a man. Suzhou is a region where many talented people assemble. Many writers and painters living in this region are involved in garden design. They are looking forward to a place full of idyllic charm comparable to that of natural landscape and famous scenery spots. Or they yearn for a site which can materialize the splendid artistic conception

构成诗情画意，将平时所见真山水、古人名迹、诗文歌句所表达的美妙意境，撷其精华而总合之，加以突出。因此，山林岩壑，一亭一榭，莫不用文学上极典雅美丽而适当的词句来形容，使游者入其地，览景而生情文，这些文字亦是对这个环境最恰当的表达。例如拙政园的远香堂与留听阁，同样是赏荷花的地方，前者出"香远益清"句，后者出"留得残荷听雨声"句。留园的闻木樨香轩，拙政园的海棠春坞，又都是根据这区所种的树木来命名的。游者至此，不期而然地能够遇见许多文学艺术的好作品，这不能不说是中国园林的一个特色了。我希望今后在许多旧园林中，如果无封建意识的文字，仅就描写风景的，应该好好保存下来。苏州诸园皆有好的题词，而怡园诸联集宋词，更能曲尽其意，可惜已经大部分不存了。至于所用材料，因园林风大，故十之八九用银杏木阴刻，填以石绿，或用木阴刻后髹漆敷色者亦有，不过色彩都是冷色。亦有用砖刻的，雅洁可爱，字体以篆、隶、行书为多，罕用正楷，取其古朴与自然。中国书画同源，本身是个艺术品，当然是会增加美观的。

树木之在园林，其重要不待细述，已所洞悉。江南园林面积小，且都属封闭性，四周绕以高垣，故对于培花植木必须深究地位之阴阳、土地之高卑、树木发育之迟速、耐寒抗旱之性能、姿态之古拙与华滋，更重要的为布置的地位与树石的安排了。园林之假山与池沼皆真山水的缩影，因此树木的配置不能任其自由发展。所栽植者必须体积不能过大，而姿态务求毕备。虬枝傍水，盘根依阿，景物遂形苍老，因此，在选树之时尤须留意此端。宜乎李格非云："人力胜者少苍古。"今日苏州树木常见的，如拙政园大树用榆；留园中部多银杏，西部则漫山枫树；怡园面积小，故易以桂、松、白皮松，尤以白皮松树虽小而姿态古拙，在小园中最是珍贵。他则杂

expressed in their poems and paintings. Therefore, they have penned the most elegant and beautiful phrases to describe the objects in a garden, including rockery, creeks, trees, hills, pavilions or halls.

These writings of couplets or tablets epitomize the fair sceneries, triggering people's passion and longing for things of beauty. For example, both the Hall of Distant Fragrance and the Stay and Listen Pavilion in the Humble Administrator's Garden are places for enjoying lotus flowers. The name "Distant Fragrance" originated from the phrase "Faint fragrance wafted from afar (香远益清)", while the name of "Stay and Listen" derived from "Listen to the rain spattering on the remnant leaves of lotus (留得残荷听雨声)". The Osmanthus Fragrance Pavilion in the Lingering Garden and the Malus Spectabilis Garden Court in the Humble Administrator's Garden are both named after the species of trees planted in the surrounding areas. It is expected that a large variety of new literary writings will be produced by those people who get inspired through journeying these sceneries. This is a unique feature of Chinese garden culture. I wish this culture would be preserved as much as possible for our future.

There is a rich collection of antithetical couplets and horizontal tablets in many of the Suzhou gardens. In the Garden of Pleasance, there are some antithetical couplets adopted from Song lyrics which express the sceneries extremely well. It is unfortunate that most of them have not survived. As regarding the material used to make couplets and tablets, due to the rough wind the majority of autographs are incised on the board of gingko and then filled with Shilü (石绿 , a special material used in autograph incision). Sometimes, the incision is covered by other cold color paint. Incisions on bricks are also seen in some gardens. They look nice and clean. Scripts such as seal script, clerical script, or semi-cursive script are the calligraphy styles used most frequently in couplets and horizontal tablets. This is because of their primitive and simple forms. On the other hand, regular script is rarely used. The Chinese calligraphy carving is an art by itself, and is of the same origin as the Chinese painting. It definitely enhances the beauty of gardens.

The importance of plants in a garden is well understood. In particular, the gardens in the region south of Yangtze are small, and most are enclosed by high walls on all sides. In selecting and cultivating flowers and plants, meticulous care should be taken of their location, sunny or shady, their position, high or low, their rate of growth, quick or slow, their resistance to cold, strong or weak, and their shape , simple or sophisticated. First priority should be given to the arrangement of plants and rockery and their compatibility with the scenery. In Chinese gardens, rockeries and ponds are a miniature of nature. Plants should be arranged with care and be prevented from growing wildly. It is important to limit their size and trim their form routinely. Otherwise, gnarled branches by the water and twisted roots around rocks will make a scene look wizend and spiritless. Once Li Gefei (李格非) said aptly: "Better effort in design can avoid a wizened and worn scene."

In Suzhou, one can find a variety of plants in different gardens. For example, elm is grown mainly as big trees in the Humble Administrator's Garden. In the Lingering Garden, gingko is frequently found in the center section while

以松、梅、棕树、黄杨，在发育上均较迟缓。园小垣高，阴地多而阳地少，于是墙阴必植耐寒植物，如女贞、棕树、竹之类，岩壑必植高山植物，如松、杉之类。阶下石隙之中，植常绿阴性草类，全园中常绿者遂多于落叶者，则四季咸青，不致秋冬髡秃无物了。至于乔木若榆、槐、枫等，除每年修枝使其姿态古拙入画外，此种树的根部甚美，尤以榆树等树龄大后，身空皮留，老干抽条，葱翠如画境。今日苏州园林中山巅栽树，大概有两种情况：第一种，山巅、山麓只植大树而虚其根部，俾可欣赏其根部与山石之美，如留园的与拙政园的一部分。第二种，山巅、山麓树木皆出丛竹或灌木之上，山石并攀以藤萝，使望去有深郁之感，如沧浪亭及拙政园的一部分。然二者设计者的依据有所不同，以我的分析，这些全在设计者所用粉本的各异，如前者师元代画家倪瓒（云林）的清逸作风，后者则效明代画家沈周（石田）的沉郁了。至于滨河低卑之地，种柳、栽竹、植芦，而墙阴栽爬山虎、修竹、天竹、秋海棠等，叶翠，花冷，实鲜，高洁耐赏，但此等亦必须每年修剪，不能任其发育。

　　园林栽花与树木同一原则，背阴且能略受阳光之地栽植桂花、山茶花之类，此二者除终年常青外，且花一在秋，一在春初，都是群花未放之时，而姿态亦佳，掩映于奇石之间，冷峻异常。紫藤则入春后一架绿荫，满树繁花，望之若珠光宝露。牡丹作台，衬以文石栏杆，实牡丹宜高地向阳，兼以其花华丽，故不得不使然。他若玉兰、海棠、牡丹、桂花等同栽庭前，谐音为玉堂富贵，当然命意已不适于今日，但对于开花的季节与色彩的安排，前人未始无理由的。桃李则宜植林，适于远眺，此在苏州，仅范围大的如留园、拙政园可以酌用之。

　　树木的布置，在苏州园林有两个原则：第一，用同一种树植之成林，

maple is spread all over the hill in its west part. The Garden of Pleasance is a small garden. Accordingly, the trees planted there include cassia, pine, and lacebark pine. In particular, the lacebark pine is small in size and assumes a simple shape. This is one of the most precious species of trees for a small garden. Other trees such as pine, plum, palm, or boxwood are also cultivated in Suzhou gardens. These trees tend to have long growth cycles. For a small garden ringed with high walls, its land lies mostly in shadow. This requires planting of cold resistant plants along the wall, such as privet, palm or bamboo. The trees chosen for high hillocks should be of the alpine type such as pine and fir. In the crevices between entrance stone steps shade-tolerant grass is the best choice. With such an arrangement, a garden will flourish with more evergreens than with deciduous trees, providing a constant source of green throughout the seasons and avoiding sterility during fall and winter. Trees such as elm, pagoda tree and maple should be trimmed annually in order to maintain its delightful and primitive shape. Their root structures are especially adorabole. A full-grown tree like elm often presents a picturesque scene by itself, with flourishing verdant twigs grown on twisted branches and a decrepit trunk.

　　In today's Suzhou gardens, there are in general two ways to plant trees on the top or the slope of a hill. One way is to plant large trees with their ground parts open. This can be found in parts of both the Lingering Garden and the Humble Administrator's Garden. Thus being done, the beauty of the tree root with rocks around it may be revealed for appreciation. The other way is to plant trees amongst bamboos or shrubs; and the rocks are covered with vines. This is the case with the Garden of Canglang Ting (the Canglang Pavilion, 沧浪亭) as well as part of the Humble Administrator's Garden. It offers a view of lushness and profundity. From my observation, these two ways of tree planting follow different ideas and originate from different painting scripts. The former complies with the style of the Yuan dynasty painter Ni Zan (Yunlin) (倪瓒 [云林]) which is noted for being fresh and elegant, while the latter abides by the style of the Ming dynasty painter Shen Zhou (Shitian) (沈周 [石田]) which is known for being lush and dark-toned. Regarding the plants in the low land along the shore, it is advisable to choose willow, bamboo, or reed. Shaded area by the wall should be covered with Japanese creeper, sacred bamboo, begonia, and slender bamboo. These types of plants with green leaves and cold colored flowers present an elegant sight. Again they need to be trimmed annually.

The principle of growing flowers and planting trees in a garden is one and the same. Osmanthus and camellia should be planted in shaded areas which receive little direct sun light. They are evergreen plants, with osmanthus flowering in autumn while camellia blooming in early spring. Both types of plants blossom before other. It is enchantingly beautiful when these fullblooming trees are rollicking among arrays of quaint-shaped rockeries. Vines such as wisteria will form a green shade over the pergola when spring begins. The multitudinous flowers sprinkled across a sprawling green look like the luster of jewelry on emerald velvet. Peony is preferably grown on a platform skirted by stone balustrade. This is because growing peony needs abundance of sun shine and high-rise land. The high location naturally enhances the magnificence of peony flower.

如怡园听涛处植松，留园西部植枫，闻木樨香轩前植桂，但又必须考虑到高低疏密间及与环境的关系。第二，用多种树同植，其配置如作画构图一样，更要注意树的方向及地的高卑是否适宜于多种树性，树叶色彩的调和对比，常绿树与落叶树的多少，开花季节的先后，树叶形态，树的姿势，树与石的关系，必须要做到片山多致、寸石生情，二者间是一个有机的联系才是。更须注意植物与建筑物的式样、颜色的衬托，是否已做到好花须映好楼台的效果。水中植荷，似不宜多，因荷多必减少了水的面积，楼台缺少倒影，故宜略点缀一二，亭亭玉立，摇曳生姿，隔秋水，宛在水中央。据云，昆山顾氏园藕植于池中石板底，石板仅凿数洞，俾不使其自由繁殖。刘师敦桢云："南京明徐氏东园池底置缸，植荷其内。"用意相同。

苏南园林以整体而论，其色彩以雅淡幽静为主，它与北方皇家园林的金碧辉煌适成对比。其所以如此，以我个人见解：第一，苏南居住建筑所施色彩在梁、枋、柱头皆用栗色，挂落用墨绿，有时柱头用黑色退光，都是一些冷色调，与白色墙面，有着强烈的对比，而花影扶疏，又适当地冲淡了墙面强白，形成良好的过渡，自多佳境了。且苏州园林皆与住宅相连，为养性读书之所，更应以清静为主，宜乎有此色调，它与北方皇家花园的那样宣扬自己威风与炫耀富贵的，在作风上有所不同。但苏州园林士大夫未始不欲炫耀富贵，然在装修、选石、陈列上用功夫，在色彩上仍然保持以雅淡为主的原则。再以南宗山水而论，水墨浅绛，略施淡彩，秀逸天成，早已印在士大夫及文人画家的脑海中，由这种思想影响下设计出来的园林，当然不会用重彩贴金了。加以江南炎热，朱红等热颜料亦在所非宜，封建社会的民居尤不能与皇家同一享受，因此色彩只好以雅静为归，用清

Traditionally, one prefers to plant magnolia, malus, peony, and osmanthus in the same courtyard since their names rhyme with the words for "jade, dignity, wealth, honor" in Chinese. Though this implication might be inadequate for today's life, the way our predecessors to reconcile the blooming periods and colors of various flowers is still worthy of appreciation. The flowering trees like peach and plum should form a grove to be viewed from afar. However, these types of trees should only be cultivated in large gardens, such as the Lingering Garden and the Humble Administrator's Garden in Suzhou.

Two principles are followed in arranging trees in Suzhou gardens. The one is to plant the same type of trees to form a grove, such as the pines at the Place of Listening to Waves in the Garden of Pleasance (怡园听涛处), the maples in the west section of the Lingering Garden, as well as the osmanthus in front of the Osmanthus Fragrance Pavilion in the Lingering Garden. While applying this principle, one should consider the height and the density of trees in relationship to the surrounding environment. The other principle is to cultivate a variety of trees. Whether it is viable or not depends on the orientation of trees and the nature of land. While selecting tree species. one should consider the contrast and balance of colors, the ratio between evergreen and deciduous trees, their blossom seasons, the shape of their leaves, and their postures. The selection of trees is indeed similar to composing a painting. The relationship between trees and rocks needs to be considered too. It is desirable to create a multitude of views along a hill, making every inch of rock scenery lively and alluring. It is also important to see to the consistency between plants and buildings in terms of the latter's forms and colors to set off each other's beauty.

Lotus needs to be planted in a pond, but in a limited way. Otherwise, the water surface would be greatly reduced with numerous lotus plants, which hinders the beautiful reflection of buildings. To adorn the water with a sprinkle of lotuses has a greater visual impact. The slim and graceful plants swaying in the middle of the pond is a perfect delight to the eye. In Gu family garden at Kunshan (昆山顾氏园), lotus was reportedly planted by placing the roots underneath stone slabs lining the pond. There are a few holes on the stone slabs allowing the plant to come through. This technique limits the propagation of the plant. Master Liu Dunzhen (刘敦桢) mentioned: "In Dongyuan of Xu family (徐氏东园) in Nanjing of the Ming dynasty, the lotus was planted by placing the roots in a vat sunk in the pond." That technique achieves the same effect of limiting lotus growth.

The main color theme of the gardens in the region south of Jiangsu is characterized by their tranquility and elegance. This is in sharp contrast to the color theme of the royal gardens in northern China, which are famed for their magnificence and splendor. In my analysis, this difference comes from several origins. First of all, the color theme of the gardens in the region south of the Jiangsu is related to the cold color theme of the local residence buildings. In this region, the column capital of a building is painted often in either chestnut or non-glossy black, and the decorative border is in dark green. The wall is white in most cases. The sharp contrast between stark black and white is toned down by tracery windows or brick-framed windows which serve as traditional

幽胜丽，设计上用少胜多的办法了。此种色彩其佳处是与整个园林轻巧的外观、灰白的江南天色、秀茂的花木、玲珑的山石、柔媚的流水，都能相配合调和，予人的感觉是淡雅幽静，这又是江南园林的特征了。

中国园林还有一个特色，就是设计者考虑到不论风雨明晦，景色咸宜，在各种自然条件下，都能予人们以最大、最舒适的美感。除山水外，而楼横堂列，廊庑回缭，栏楯周接，木映花承，是起了最大的作用的，给人们提供了在各种自然条件下来欣赏园林的条件。诗人、画家在各种不同的境界中，产生了各种不同的体会，如夏日的蕉廊，冬日的梅影、雪月，春日的繁花、丽日，秋日的红蓼、芦塘，虽四时之景不同，而景物无不适人。至于松风听涛，菰蒲闻雨，月移花影，雾失楼台，斯景又宜其览者自得之。这种效果的产生，主要是设计者对文学艺术的高度修养而与实际的建筑相结合，使理想中的境界付之于实现，并撷其最佳者渲染扩大。因此，叠石构屋，凿水穿泉，栽花种竹，都是向这个目标前进的。文学家、艺术家对自然美的欣赏不仅是一个春日的艳阳天气，他们对任何一个季节时间，都要将之变成美的境地。因此，在花影考虑到粉墙，听风考虑到松，听雨考虑到荷叶，月色考虑到柳梢，斜阳考虑到漏窗，岁寒考虑到梅竹，等等，都希望理想中的幻景而付诸实现。故其安排一石一木，都寄托了丰富的情感，宜乎处处有情，面面生意，含蓄有曲折，余味不尽了。此又为中国园林的特征。

以上所述，系就个人所见，掇拾一二，提供大家参考。我相信，苏州园林不但在中国造园史上有其重要与光辉的一页，同时今日尚为广大人民作游憩之所。我们如何继承与发挥优良的文化传统，此份资料似有提出的必要。当然管见所及，定多不妥，还希望大家予以指正。

structures. Many spectacular scenes have been created out of this design.

Indeed, almost all the Suzhou gardens were originally attached to residential houses for the purpose of providing a quiet place for study and self cultivation. This motivation sets the tone for the cold color scheme. Consequently, the design philosophy of Suzhou gardens is obviously different from that of northern royal gardens which was intended to demonstrate the royal power and opulence. In contrast, the scholar-officials in Suzhou showed off their affluence through refined furnishing, meticulous rockery selection as well as exquisite exhibition in their gardens while maintaining a tasteful style of light and cool colors.

The preference to cold color theme in Suzhou gardens resulted also from the influence of paintings in this region. The natural landscape paintings in southern China are composed of strokes of dark shades accompanied by touches of few light colors. This natural and elegant style is imprinted on the mind of scholars, writers, and artists of the region. Its influence leads the garden design away from use of exuberant and glossy gold colors. In addition, since it is extremely hot during summer in the south of the Yangtze River, the rich colors such as red do not fit well. Furthermore, the commoners in the feudal times were not allowed to enjoy the same life style as royal households. The color scheme is consequently limited to those that are light and quiet. One must use a quiet and elegant design to outshine the lavish excess, and use few to outmatch many. This cold color scheme is in harmony with the exterior look of Suzhou gardens: cloudy sky, flourishing trees, exquisite rockeries, as well as the gentle flow of water, which together creates a sense of tranquility and elegance. This is one of the unique features of the gardens in the South of Yangtze region.

Another peculiar feature of all Chinese gardens is that they should be designed in such a way that under any natural conditions, rainy or shiny and at dawn or at dusk, their scenery invariably gives maximum sense of comfort and pleasure. However, without well-planned halls and pavilions, well-made verandas and balustrades, well-arranged trees and flowers in addition to well-wrought rockeries and brooks, sceneries can hardly be appreciated in various natural conditions.

Different circumstances can evoke different feelings in the mind of poets or writers. Plantain shaded veranda in summer, sturdy plum and moon light on snow in winter, sunlight and flowers in spring, red knotweed and reed-ringed ponds in fall, these scenes vary with seasons, but are all enjoyable. The rustling of wind through pines, the spattering of rain on wild rice and sweet flags, the swaying flower shadows under the moon, and the fog-cloaked towers, these are all scenes that can elicit different emotions from different people. Garden designers should rely on their profound knowledge in art and literature and base themselves on actual environment to create a garden that can trigger all these human reactions to its scenerises through glamorizing and exaggerating the effect of the most outsanding features. For this purpose, the materialization of a dreamland, they should exert themselves to do whatever they can, laying rocks, raising buildings, channeling water and cultivating plants.

An artist or a man of letters does not indulge in the splendor of spring days only, but has also learnt to enjoy other seasons. They should resort to different ways to ferret out the beauty of each possible circumstance. Watching the swaying flower shadows, they are thinking of what they could do on a whitewashed wall. Listening to the sound of wind, they are imagining the rustling pine trees, Pattering rain revokes pearls jumping and rolling on lotus leaves. Lucid moon reminds them of the moonlight-touched tops of swinging willows. Sunset prompts them to twilight radiating through a tracery window. Year-end cold endears them to the sturdy plum and slender bamboo. They instill their passion in every rock and every plant in order to realize their dreamland. Therefore, in a Chinese garden, every corner is imbued with a sentiment and every side exudes a meaning. It leaves a lasting and pleasant aftertaste. This is all it means for a Chinese garden.

I have put together my own observations here to provide readers a reference to Suzhou gardens. It is my belief that the value of gardens in Suzhou should not just be an important and illustrious page in the history of Chinese gardens. It should still be appreciated as a place of recreation and cultivation for the people. The material presented here is instrumental in understanding what we can do to foster the splendid culture tradition we have inherited. There may be some inadequacies in my personal observations. Any criticism or suggestion is welcome.

In the heaven's breath,
under the silvery moonlight,
lie a hill and a dale defying
nature's might. On the
human's earth, against age
old plight and slight, stand
still a few bowers and towers
basking in brilliant sunlight.

风月一丘壑
今古几楼台

拙政园大门

Front gate of Zhuozheng Yuan (the Humble Administrator's Garden)

小院深明别有天

拙政园自别有洞天东望

Center section of Zhuozheng Yuan (the Humble Administrator's
Garden), viewed through Bieyoudongtian (a moon gate with a
special name of Another Cave World)

Cloud-scraping rocks.

拙政园自腰门内望

View of Zhuozheng Yuan (the Humble Administrator's
Garden) from Yaomen (side gate of the Garden)

拙政园绣绮亭及云墙

Xiuqi Ting (the Paeonia Suffruticosa Pavilion) and Yunqiang (the Undulating Wall) in Zhuozheng Yuan (the Humble Administrator's Garden)

远香堂环境图
| Site Plan of Yuanxiang Tang (the Hall of Distant Fragrance)

远香堂平面图
| Floor plan of Yuanxiang Tang (the Hall of Distant Fragrance)

What on earth a wondrous
spring can bring: Blooming
flowers sway and willow
branches swing.

拙政园自绣绮亭俯视远香堂及倚玉轩
Yuanxiang Tang (the Hall of Distant Fragrance) and Yiyu Xuan (the
Bamboo Pavilion) in Zhuozheng Yuan (the Humble Administrator's
Garden), viewed from Xiuqi Ting (the Paeonia Suffruticosa Pavilion)

远香堂正立面图
| Front elevation of Yuanxiang Tang (the Hall of Distant Fragrance)

远香堂侧立面图
| Side elevation of Yuanxiang Tang (the Hall of Distant Fragrance)

Of a dreamland i am forever fond: by the peony-skirted pavilion and breeze creased pond.

临水最相宜
东风吹绣猗

拙政园绣绮亭、远香堂及倚玉轩

Xiuqi Ting (the Paeonia Suffruticosa Pavilion), Yuanxiang Tang (the Hall of Distant Fragrance) and Yiyu Xuan (the Bamboo Pavilion) in Zhuozheng Yuan (the Humble Administrator's Garden)

Through the marble moon
gate spring sprightly comes,
Flowering raspberry
outshines fading crab apple
blossoms.

拙政园自枇杷园望雪香云蔚亭

Xuexiangyunwei Ting (the Snow-Like Fragrant Prunus Mume
Pavilion) in Zhuozheng Yuan (the Humble Administrator's
Garden), viewed throught the entrance Moon Gate of Pipa
Yuan (Loquat Garden Court)

庭院深深深幾許

拙政园枇杷园入口
Entrance of Pipa Yuan (Loquat Garden Court) in Zhuozheng
Yuan (the Humble Administrator's Garden)

绣绮亭平面图
| Floor plan of Xiuqi Ting (the Paeonia Suffruticosa Pavililon)

Floating clouds and swaying leaves cast fleeting shadows; The singing of crickes is wafting in the fragrant willows.

拙政园绣绮亭

Xiuqi Ting (the Paeonia Suffruticosa Pavilion) in Zhuozheng Yuan (the Humble Administrator's Garden)

绣绮亭立面图
| Elevation of Xiuqi Ting (the Paeonia Suffruticosa Pavilion)

绣绮亭横断面图
| Cross section of Xiuqi Ting (the Paeonia Suffruticosa Pavilion)

During the day the sun shines on the shut window, toward the eve the screen hangs still and low.

拙政园玲珑馆及绣绮亭

Linglong Guan (the Hall of Elegance) and Xiuqi Ting (the Paeonia Suffruticosa Pavilion) in Zhuozheng Yuan (the Humble Administrator's Garden)

倚虹亭

海棠春坞

玲珑馆

玲珑馆及海棠春坞环境图
| Site plan of Linglong Guan (the Hall of Elegance) and
Haitangchunwu (the Malus Spectabilis Garden Court)

玲珑馆平面图
| Floor plan of Linglong Guan (the Hall of Elegance)

玲珑馆正立面图
| Front elevation of Linglong Guan (the Hall of Elegance)

玲珑馆侧立面图
| Side elevation of Linglong Guan (the Hall of Elegance)

In the spacious yard all
is still and quiet;
in the small pavilion no
one is in sight.

拙政园海棠春坞

Haitangchunwu (the Malus Spectabilis Garden Court)
in Zhuozheng Yuan (the Humble Administrator's Garden)

海棠春坞正立面图
| Front elevation of Haitangchunwu (the Malus Spectabilis Garden Court)

海棠春坞平面图
| Floor plan of Haitangchunwu (the Malus Spectabilis Garden Court)

By the painted rails and
along the tranquil trails,
The aroma of crab apple
blossoms suffuses your
folds and frills.

画阑幽径
又海棠开了
香满衣襟

拙政园海棠春坞入口
Entrance of Haitangchunwu (the Malus Spectabilis Garden Court) in
Zhuozheng Yuan (the Humble Administrator's Garden)

The day is sluggish in passing: the crab-apple blossoms are found withering.

海棠花謝也
日遲遲

拙政园海棠春坞

Haitangchunwu (the Malus Spectabilis Garden Court) in Zhuozheng Yuan (the Humble Administrator's Garden)

隔院樓臺

拙政园海棠春坞漏窗
Lattice Window in Haitangchunwu (the Malus Spectabilis Garden Court) of Zhuozheng Yuan (the Humble Administrator's Garden)

91

倚虹亭正立面图
| Front elevation of Yihong Ting (Leaning Against Rainbow Pavilion)

倚虹亭平面图
| Floor plan of Yihong Ting (Leaning Against Rainbow Pavilion)

A stream is gurgling on and on.
Colored petals keep parachuting
down and down. Watching on the
bridge catkins floating around,
the green turning greener I've
ever found.

拙政园倚虹桥及海棠春坞背面
Yihong Qiao (Leaning Against Rainbow Bridge) and the back
of Haitangchunwu (the Malus Spectabilis Garden Court) in
Zhuozheng Yuan (the Humble Administrator's Garden)

The oblique twilight lingers
on the winding rail;
The recess of willow grove
remains outside its pale.

拙政园自倚虹亭望远香堂及倚玉轩背部

Yuanxiang Tang (the Hall of Distant Fragrance) and back of Yiyu Xuan (the
Bamboo Pavilion) in Zhuozheng Yuan (the Humble Administrator's Garden),
viewed from Yihong Ting (Leaning Against Rainbow Pavilion)

Spring has not yet
tinged the woods
green; I lean on the
rail to sketch its quiet
scene.

拙政园自倚虹亭西望

Center section of Zhuozheng Yuan (the Humble
Administrator's Garden), viewed from Yihong Ting (Leaning
Against Rainbow Pavilion)

梧竹幽居正立面图
| Front elevation of Wuzhuyouju (the Secluded Pavilion of Firmiana Simplex and Bamboo)

梧竹幽居平面图
| Floor plan of Wuzhuyouju (the Secluded Pavilion of Firmiana Simplex and Bamboo)

A glimpse of beauty
through the ring-shaped
moon gate.

拙政园梧竹幽居

Wuzhuyouju (the Secluded Pavilion of Firmiana Simplex and
Bamboo) in Zhuozheng Yuan (the Humble Administrator's
Garden)

1. 绿漪亭
| Lüyi Ting
2. 梧竹幽居
| Wuzhuyouju

梧竹幽居及绿漪亭环境图
| Site plan of Wuzhuyouju (the Secluded Pavilion of Firmiana Simplex and Bamboo) and Lüyi Ting (the Green Ripple Pavilion)

The Moon gate echoed with spring.

拙政园梧竹幽居望绿漪亭

Lüyi Ting (the Green Ripple Pavilion) in Zhuozheng Yuan
(the Humble Administrator's Garden), viewed from Wuzhuyouju (the
Secluded Pavilion of Firmiana Simplex and Bamboo)

绿漪亭正立面图
| Front elevation of Lüyi Ting (the Green Ripple Pavilion)

绿漪亭平面图
| Floor plan of Lüyi Ting (the Green Ripple Pavilion)

Poplars and willows grow
lush and green,
sprinkling the mini
ripples with verdant
sheen.

杨柳绿成阴
流水澈々照影

拙政园绿漪亭望三曲桥

Sanqu Qiao (the Three Fold Zigzag Bridge) in Zhuozheng
Yuan (the Humble Administrator's Garden), viewed from
Lüyi Ting (the Green Ripple Pavilion)

待霜亭环境图
| Site plan of Daishuang Ting (the Orange Pavilion)

待霜亭正立面图
| Front elevation of Daishuang Ting
(the Orange Pavilion)

待霜亭平面图
| Floor plan of Daishuang Ting (the
Orange Pavilion)

West of long corridor, long
and oder rich, there lies a
red painted mini bridge.

长廊西畔小红桥

拙政园自绿漪亭望梧竹幽居
Wuzhuyouju (the Secluded Pavilion of Firmiana Simplex and
Bamboo) in Zhuozheng Yuan (the Humble Administrator's Garden),
viewed from Lüyi Ting (the Green Ripple Pavilion)

Whirling water winding along the wild deep dale.

乱山深處水瀠洄

拙政园梧竹幽居

Wuzhuyouju (the Secluded Pavilion of Firmiana Simplex and Bamboo) in Zhuozheng Yuan (the Humble Administrator's Garden)

The green hills are so
bewitching; the silvery
moon is so beguiling; both
vie with each other for me
inviting.

拙政园待霜亭及梧竹幽居

Daishuang Ting (the Orange Pavilion) and Wuzhuyouju (the Secluded
Pavilion of Firmiana Simplex and Bamboo) in Zhuozheng Yuan (the
Humble Administrator's Garden)

雪香云蔚亭环境图
| Site plan of Xuexiangyunwei Ting (the
Snow-Like Fragrant Prunus Mume Pavilion)

雪香云蔚亭正立面图
| Front elevation of Xuexiangyunwei Ting
(the Snow-Like Fragrant Prunus Mume
Pavilion)

雪香云蔚亭侧立面图
| Side elevation of Xuexiangyunwei Ting
(the Snow-Like Fragrant Prunus Mume
Pavilion)

The wide water mirrors
the wide sky. The still
trees stand in the still air.

天宽水也宽
风静林还静

拙政园自远香堂望雪香云蔚亭

Xuexiangyunwei Ting (the Snow-Like Fragrant Prunus
Mume Pavilion) in Zhuozheng Yuan (the Humble
Administrator's Garden), viewed from Yuanxiang Tang (the
Hall of Distant Fragrance)

雪香云蔚亭正立面与环境图
| Front elevation and the surroundings of Xuexiangyunwei Ting
(the Snow-Like Fragrant Prunus Mume Pavilion)

雪香云蔚亭横断面图
| Cross Section of Xuexiangyunwei Ting
(the Snow-Like Fragrant Prunus Mume Pavilion)

Verdant shades with the long
spring day stays swelling
streams under the arched
bridge flew all the way, and
around the petty curtained
tower joyfully play.

拙政园自雪香云蔚亭下西南望倚玉轩及香洲

Yiyu Xuan (the Bamboo Pavilion) and Xiangzhou
(the Fragrant Isle) in Zhuozheng Yuan (the Humble Administrator's Garden),
viewed from Xuexiangyunwei Ting (the Snow-Like Fragrant Prunus Mume
Pavilion)

Along the trails red flowers grow sparse; across the fields far and wide spread green grass.

小径红稀
芳郊绿遍

拙政园曲径小桥（译者注：这是连接待霜亭和
雪香云蔚亭所在的两个小岛的小桥。）

Winding trail and pedestrian stone bridge in Zhuozheng Yuan (the
Humble Administrator's Garden). (Note by translator: This is the bridge
connecting the two islets where the Orange Pavilion and the Snow-Like
Fragrant Prunus Mume Pavilion are located respectively.)

Along the wall a hedge of
bamboo treads from
bunches of flowers
scented warmth spreads.

繞牆深叢竹
花氣烘人尚暖

拙政园云墙及铺地

Yunqiang (the Undulating Wall) and the patterned pavement in
Zhuozheng Yuan (the Humble Administrator's Garden)

见山楼环境图
| Site plan of Jianshan Lou (the Mountain-In-View Tower)

The winding rails are
entangled with red rose;
The upturned eaves are
hanging emerald in the air.
Of all these who on earth
knows? Only the jade
balustrade is aware.

看檻曲縈紅
檐牙飛翠
惟有玉闌知

拙政园自玉兰堂北望见山楼

Jianshan Lou (the Mountain-In-View Tower) in Zhuozheng Yuan
(the Humble Administrator's Garden), viewed from Yulan Tang (the
Magnolia Hall)

见山楼正立面图
| Front elevation of Jianshan Lou
(the Mountain-In-View Tower)

The pavilion permeated with the fragrance of fallen plum blossom, the pond painted emerald by the grass tender and lilies me.

落梅亭榭香
芳草池塘綠

拙政园自别有洞天望见山楼及五曲桥

Jianshan Lou (the Mountain-In-View Tower) and Wuqu Qiao (Five Fold Zigzag Bridge) in Zhuozheng Yuan (the Humble Administrator's Garden), viewed from Bieyoudongtian (a moon gate with a special name of Another Cave World)

见山楼二层平面图
| Floor plan of the first floor of Jianshan Lou
 (the Mountain-In-View Tower)

见山楼底层平面图
| Floor plan of the ground floor of Jianshan Lou
 (the Mountain-In-View Tower)

Under the rainbow bridge
gently runs the silvery
stream; pearly drops of rain
on the leaves sparkle in the
slanting sun's gleam.

流水畫橋畔
兩餘芳草斜陽

拙政园见山楼侧面
Jianshan Lou (the Mountain-In-View Tower) in Zhuozheng
Yuan (the Humble Administrator's Garden)

见山楼侧立面图
| Side elevation of Jianshan Lou
(the Mountain-In-View Tower)

长虹卧碧
斜阳低尽柳如烟

拙政园见山楼侧面及五曲桥

Wuqu Qiao (Five Fold Zigzag Bridge) and a corner of
Jianshan Lou (the Mountain-In-View Tower) in Zhuozheng
Yuan (the Humble Administrator's Garden)

见山楼背立面图
| Back elevation of Jianshan Lou
(the Mountain-In-View Tower)

Beyond the mist, lovely
flowers don the red of light
shade; outside the rail,
thickets of bush dot the rocks
artfully laid.

烟外好花红浅淡
槛前叠石翠参差

拙政园见山楼背面

Backside of Jianshan Lou (the Mountain-In-View Tower)
in Zhuozheng Yuan (the Humble Administrator's Garden)

嘉实亭正立面图
| Front elevation of Jiashi Ting
(the Loquat Pavilion)

嘉实亭平面图
| Floor plan of Jiashi Ting
(the Loquat Pavilion)

As the fog lifts, a multi
tier bower looms large
and near; a winding rail
runs along a curved pond
lucid and clear.

拙政园见山楼背面爬山廊

Roofed walkway at the backside of Jianshan Lou (the
Mountain-In-View Tower) in Zhuozheng Yuan (the Humble
Administrator's Garden)

With zigzag rails the
lengthy corridor is sieged;
In greenish yellow the
slender willow twigs are
tinged.

拙政园柳荫路曲长廊

Veranda of Liuyinluqu (A Winding Way with Willow Shades) in
Zhuozheng Yuan (the Humble Administrator's Garden)

小院迴廊春已滿
水閣無塵午晝長

拙政园见山楼下
Ground level of Jianshan Lou (the Mountain-In-View Tower)
in Zhuozheng Yuan (the Humble Administrator's Garden)

香洲环境图
| Site plan of Xiangzhou (the Fragrant Isle)

1. 香洲 | Xiangzhou
2. 得真亭 | Dezhen Ting
3. 一庭秋月啸松风亭
| Yitingqiuyuexiaosongfeng Ting

香洲（一层）及澂观楼（二层）平面图
| Floor plans of Xiangzhou (the Fragrant Isle, ground
floor) and Chengguan Lou (Clear Water Viewing Tower, first floor)

The bower stands tall over
an expanse of pond;
The rain breathes coolness
before it comes around.

高閣對橫塘
水亭未雨涼先覺

拙政园香洲
Xiangzhou (the Fragrant Isle) in Zhuozheng Yuan (the
Humble Administrator's Garden)

香洲及澄观楼侧立面图
| Side elevation of Xiangzhou (the Fragrant Isle)
and Chengguan Lou (Clear Water Viewing Tower)

Around the bower faint
fragrance flows; sprouting
buds green willow's
tips and tops.

暗香来水阁
花枝破芽柳梢青

拙政园香洲
Xiangzhou (the Fragrant Isle) in Zhuozheng Yuan
(the Humble Administrator's Garden)

香洲及澂观楼正立面图
| Front elevation of Xiangzhou (the Fragrant Isle)
and Chengguan Lou (Clear Water Viewing Tower)

The pavilion is fenced by
lines of willow lush and
luxuriant; the pond is
flanked by carpets of grass
perfuming and pliant.

拙政园自柳荫路曲望倚玉轩及香洲

Yiyu Xuan (the Bamboo Pavilion) and Xiangzhou (the Fragrant Isle) in
Zhuozheng Yuan (the Humble Administrator's Garden), viewed from
Liuyinluqu (A Winding Way with Willow Shades)

秋風清
秋月明
竹外松邊
秋景如畫

The autumn air is fresh; the autumn moon is bright. The pine trees nestle in the bamboo bush; so infatuating the scene is in sight.

拙政园小飞虹及一庭秋月啸松风亭

Xiaofeihong (the Small Flying Rainbow Bridge) and
Yitingqiuyuexiaosongfeng Ting (Autumn Moon and Windy Pine Pavilion)
in Zhuozheng Yuan (the Humble Administrator's Garden)

小沧浪正立面图
| Front elevation of Xiaocanglang
(the Small Canglang)

小沧浪平面图
| Floor plan of Xiaocanglang
(the Small Canglang)

小沧浪横断面图
| Cross section of Xiaocanglang
(the Small Canglang)

The crowd on the land cast
their shadow in the pond;
the cloud in the air in silvery
water is found. In the sky
floats the cloud; in the cloud
move the crowd.

溪边照影行
天在清溪底
天上有行云
人在行云裏

拙政园自小沧浪北望荷风四面亭及见山楼

Hefengsimian Ting (the Pavilion in Lotus Breezes) and Jianshan Lou (the
Mountain-In-View Tower) in Zhuozheng Yuan (the Humble Administrator's
Garden), viewed from Xiaocanglang (the Small Canglang)

一庭秋月啸松风亭立面图
| Elevation of Yitingqiuyuexiaosongfeng Ting
(Autumn Moon and Windy Pine Pavilion)

一庭秋月啸松风亭平面图
| Floor plan of Yitingqiuyuexiaosongfeng Ting
(Autumn Moon and Windy Pine Pavilion)

Waterside pavilion
delights in the shade
of spring flowers.

拙政园一庭秋月啸松风亭

Yitingqiuyuexiaosongfeng Ting (Autumn Moon and
Windy Pine Pavilion) in Zhuozheng Yuan (the Humble
Administrator's Garden)

得真亭正立面图
| Front elevation of Dezhen Ting (the True Nature Pavilion)

得真亭平面图
| Floor plan of Dezhen Ting (the True Nature Pavilion)

A solitary man wades
through petals fallen;
A pair of swallows hovers
on drizzly breeze arisen.

落花人獨立
微雨燕雙飛

拙政园得真亭

De ZhenTing (the True Nature Pavilion) in Zhuozheng Yuan (the
Humble Administrator's Garden)

倚玉轩正立面图
| Front elevation of Yiyu Xuan (the Bamboo Pavilion)

倚玉轩侧立面图
| Side elevation of Yiyu Xuan (the Bamboo Pavilion)

倚玉轩平面图
| Floor plan of Yiyu Xuan (the Bamboo Pavilion)

What a cool place! the path is paved with fallen petals; the pond brims over with silver ripples.

有此清凉界
落红铺径水平池

拙政园倚玉轩

Yiyu Xuan (the Bamboo Pavilion) in Zhuozheng Yuan (the Humble Administrator's Garden)

A tree skirted pond afloat
with fallen flowers.

落花浮水　樹臨池

拙政园荷风四面亭

Hefengsimian Ting (the Pavilion in Lotus Breezes) in
Zhuozheng Yuan (the Humble Administrator's Garden)

荷风四面亭正立面图
| Front elevation of Hefengsimian Ting (the Pavilion in Lotus Breezes)

荷风四面亭平面图
| Floor plan of Hefengsimian Ting (the Pavilion in Lotus Breezes)

Vernal breeze caresses
the pond rippling but
clear water sieged
bower watches over the
dyke near and dear.

春透水波明
池上楼台堤上路

拙政园荷风四面亭及见山楼

Hefengsimian Ting (the Pavilion in Lotus Breezes) and Jianshan
Lou (the Mountain-In-View Tower) in Zhuozheng Yuan (the
Humble Administrator's Garden)

荷风四面亭环境图
| Site plan of Hefengsimian Ting (the Pavilion in Lotus Breezes)

Lithe and wispy twigs coil and swing in the sky azure; oblique rays of twilight shine upon the willow tops to allure.

游丝捲晴画
斜阳微放柳梢明

拙政园荷风四面亭

Hefengsimian Ting (the Pavilion in Lotus Breezes) in
Zhuozheng Yuan (the Humble Administrator's Garden)

The day dawns fair and bright, with breeze blowing soft and light.

晴景初升風細細

拙政园柳荫路曲长廊（未修理前）

Veranda of Liuyinluqu (A Winding Way with Willow Shades), before repair, in Zhuozheng Yuan (the Humble Administrator's Garden)

浮翠阁横断面图
| Cross Section of Fucui Ge (the Floating Green Tower)

浮翠阁正立面图
| Front elevation of Fucui Ge (the Floating Green Tower)

浮翠阁底层平面图
| Floor plan of the ground floor of Fucui Ge
(the Floating Green Tower)

玉兰堂正立面图
| Front elevation of Yulan Tang (the Magnolia Hall)

玉兰堂平面图
| Floor plan of Yulan Tang (the Magnolia Hall)

In the sky the sun
holds sway; behind the
fence the shadow shies
away.

拙政园玉兰堂前

Front of Yulan Tang (the Magnolia Hall) in Zhuozheng Yuan
(the Humble Administrator's Garden)

别有洞天

别有洞天环境图
| Site plan of Bieyoudongtian (a moon gate with a special name of
Another Cave World)

In the shade verdant,
warblers are singing with
melodious sound;
In the woods around,
remnant petals can no
longer be found.

啼嬌聲在綠陰中
無處覓殘紅

拙政园别有洞天

Bieyoudongtian (a moon gate with a special name of Another Cave
World) in Zhuozheng Yuan (the Humble Administrator's Garden)

别有洞天正立面图
| Front elevation of Bieyoudongtian (a moon gate with a special name of Another Cave World)

别有洞天平面图
| Floor plan of Bieyoudongtian (a moon gate with a special name of Another Cave World)

A fog-cloaked tower.

雾失楼臺

拙政园自别有洞天东望五曲桥

Wuqu Qiao (Five Fold Zigzag Bridge) in Zhuozheng Yuan
(the Humble Administrator's Garden), viewed from Bieyoudongtian (a
moon gate with a special name of Another Cave World)

A long winded corridor
meanders its way in fall fair:
A nearby stream is gurgling
among the boulders bare.

秋
水
長
廊
水
石
間

拙政园水廊

Shuilang (Winding Veranda over the Water) in Zhuozheng
Yuan (the Humble Administrator's Garden)

Graceful bamboo
in a harmony with
grotesque boulder.

疏筠怪石相宜

拙政园水廊自北向南望

Shuilang (Winding Veranda over the Water) in
Zhuozheng Yuan (the Humble Administrator's Garden),
viewed from north end

倒影楼

倒影楼环境图
| Site plan of Daoying Lou (the Tower of Reflection)

Towers and towers
wreathed with fragrant
flowers waving.
Steps and terraces
shrouded by pliable
plantain roving.

臺榭繞崖芳
芭蕉籠碧砌

拙政园水廊自南向北望

Shuilang (Winding Veranda over the Water)
in Zhuozheng Yuan (the Humble Administrator's Garden),
viewed from south end

倒影楼正立面图
| Front elevation of Daoying Lou (the Tower of Reflection)

倒影楼侧立面图
| Side elevation of Daoying Lou (the Tower of Reflection)

Myriads of slender twigs of willow in the vernal wind sway and flow, touching tenderly the tower and swinging shreds of shade on the pond shallow.

万条杨柳风
高拂楼台低映水

拙政园水廊及倒影楼

Shuilang (Winding Veranda over the Water) and Daoying Lou (the Tower of Reflection) in Zhuozheng Yuan (the Humble Administrator's Garden)

倒影楼（二层）平面图
| First floor plan of Daoying Lou (the Tower of Reflection)

倒影楼一层（拜文揖沈之斋）平面图
| Ground floor plan of Daoying Lou (Baiwenyishenzhi Zhai,
the Room for Worshipping Wen and Shen)

The moonshine sneaks
up the steps of a yard
 stefand, shedding stripes
of shadow on the railed
ground.

庭院无人月上阶
满地阑干影

拙政园拜文揖沈之斋（倒影楼下层）

Baiwenyishenzhi Zhai (the Room for Worshipping Wen and Shen,
ground floor of Daoying Lou [The Tower of Reflection]) in Zhuozheng
Yuan (the Humble Administrator's Garden)

宜两亭立面图
| Front elevation of Yiliang Ting
 (the Good for Both Families Pavilion)

宜两亭平面图
| Floor plan of Yiliang Ting
 (the Good for Both Families Pavilion)

A pavilion on wind
wrinkled water.

水館風亭

拙政园拜文揖沈之斋（倒影楼下层）望宜两亭

View of Yiliang Ting (the Good for Both Families Pavilion) through a window in
Baiwenyishenzhi Zhai (the Room for Worshipping Wen and Shen, ground floor
of Daoying Lou [The Tower of Reflection]) in Zhuozheng Yuan (the Humble
Administrator's Garden)

1. 十八曼陀罗花馆 | Shiba Mantuoluohua Guan (the Hall of Eighteen Camellias)

2. 三十六鸳鸯馆 | Sanshiliu Yuanyang Guan (the Hall of Thirty-six Pairs of Mandarin Ducks)

3. 塔影亭 | Taying Ting (the Pagoda Reflection Pavilion)

4. 留听阁 | Liuting Ge (the Stay and Listen Pavilion)

5. 宜两亭 | Yiliang Ting (the Good for Both Families Pavilion)

三十六鸳鸯馆环境图
| Site plan of Sanshiliu Yuanyang Guan
(the Hall of Thirty-six Pairs of Mandarin Ducks)

In the quiet, sun bathed
yard and along the winding
corridor, I amble in
leisure, looking for flowers
in their splendor.

日長深院悄
起尋花影步迴廊

拙政园三十六鸳鸯馆东面入口

East entrance of Sanshiliu Yuanyang Guan (the Hall of
Thirty-six Pairs of Mandarin Ducks) in Zhuozheng Yuan (the
Humble Administrator's Garden)

三十六鸳鸯馆曲廊平面图
| Floor plan of winding veranda of Sanshiliu Yuanyang Guan (the Hall of Thirty-six Pairs of Mandarin Ducks)

三十六鸳鸯馆曲廊屋顶仰视图
| Ceiling plan of winding veranda of Sanshiliu Yuanyang Guan (the Hall of Thirty-six Pairs of Mandarin Ducks)

Full bloomed roses fiddling
with the window,
Diffusing into the hall air
fresh and mellow.

拙政园三十六鸳鸯馆东面入口

East entrance of Sanshiliu Yuanyang Guan (the Hall of Thirty-six Pairs of Mandarin Ducks) in Zhuozheng Yuan (the Humble Administrator's Garden)

三十六鸳鸯馆曲廊透视图
| Perspective view of winding veranda of of Sanshiliu Yuanyang Guan (the Hall of Thirty-six Pairs of Mandarin Ducks)

The trees are weighed down
with wax but their charms
and features remain.
The yard is tranquil and
there ain't the leoud
their chon at table more can
can enish.

拙政园三十六鸳鸯馆西面入口

West entrance of Sanshiliu Yuanyang Guan (the Hall of Thirty-six Paris of Mandarin Ducks) in Zhuozheng Yuan (the Humble Administrator's Garden)

三十六鸳鸯馆临水立面图
| Water side elevation of Sanshiliu Yuanyang Guan
(the Hall of Thirty-six Pairs of Mandarin Ducks)

三十六鸳鸯馆及十八曼陀罗花馆平面图
| Floor plan of Sanshiliu Yuanyang Guan (the Hall of Thirty-six
Pairs of Mandarin Ducks) and Shiba Mantuoluohua Guan (the
Hall of Eighteen Camellias)

Twilight sets ripples sparking
for miles and miles around;
A pair of loverbirds are
sporting on a wavy carpet of a
pond.

水底明霞十顷光
天教铺锦衬鸳鸯

拙政园留听阁与三十六鸳鸯馆

Liuting Ge (the Stay and Listen Pavilion) and SanshiliuYuanyang
Guan (the Hall of Thirty-six Pairs of Mandarin Ducks) in Zhuozheng
Yuan (the Humble Administrator's Garden)

三十六鸳鸯馆及十八曼陀罗花馆侧立面图
| Side elevation of Sanshiliu Yuanyang Guan (the Hall of Thirty-
six Pairs of Mandarin Ducks) and Shiba Mantuoluohua Guan
(the Hall of Eighteen Camellias)

三十六鸳鸯馆及十八曼陀罗花馆横断面图
| Cross section of Sanshiliu Yuanyang Guan (the Hall of Thirty-
six Pairs of Mandarin Ducks) and Shiba Mantuoluohua Guan
(the Hall of Eighteen Camellias)

Spring day has come to
stay, and loath it go away.

拙政园三十六鸳鸯馆

Sanshiliu Yuanyang Guan (the Hall of Thirty-six Pairs of Mandarin
Ducks) in Zhou Zheng Yuan (the Humble Administrator's Garden)

The petty pavilion cuddles up
in misty willows;
The soothing stream gently
and quietly flows.

拙政园笠亭

Liting (the Bamboo Hat Pavilion) in Zhuozheng Yuan (the
Humble Administrator's Garden)

日長風靜
花影閒相照。

拙政园扇亭山石

Rockeries at Shanting (the Fan Pavilion, also called
Yusheitongzuo Xuan ["With Whom Shall I Sit?" Pavilion])
in Zhuozheng Yuan (the Humble Administrator's Garden)

笠亭立面图

| Elevation of Liting (the Bamboo Hat Pavilion)

笠亭平面图

| Floor plan of Liting (the Bamboo Hat Pavilion)

What a delight!
Leaning on the ceiling
vine by the waterside,
Or ascending the green
hill with springy stride.

倚藤临水
步屟登山

拙政园笠亭

Liting (the Bamboo Hat Pavilion) in Zhuozheng Yuan (the
Humble Administrator's Garden)

与谁同坐轩正立面图
| Front elevation of Yusheitongzuo Xuan
("With Whom Shall I Sit?" Pavilion)

与谁同坐轩平面图
| Floor plan of Yusheitongzuo Xuan
("With Whom Shall I Sit?" Pavilion)

The bower astride the brook,
crystal and purling;
The water without rippling
and the wind subsiding;
Upside down in the water
mirror flowers blooming.

拙政园扇亭及三十六鸳鸯馆

Shanting (the Fan Pavilion, also called Yusheitongzuo Xuan ["With Whom Shall I Sit?" Pavilion]) and Sanshiliu Yuanyang Guan (the Hall of Thirty-six Pairs of Mandarin Ducks) in Zhuozheng Yuan (the Humble Administrator's Garden)

与谁同坐轩侧立面图
| Side elevation of Yusheitongzuo Xuan
("With Whom Shall I Sit?" Pavilion)

Blossom hemmed bower
and willow wreathed gate.

花間亭館柳間門

拙政园自扇亭望三十六鸳鸯馆

Sanshiliu Yuanyang Guan (the Hall of Thirty-six Pairs
of Mandarin Ducks) in Zhuozheng Yuan (the Humble
Administrator's Garden), viewed from Shanting (the Fan
Pavilion, also called "With Whom Shall I Sit ?" Pavilion)

With whom to share such a
splendid night?
The crescent moon, cool
breeze and me on site.

拙政园扇亭窗

Window in Shanting (the Fan Pavilion) in Zhuozheng Yuan (the Humble
Administrator's Garden). The Chinese characters on the inscribed
plaque hung above the window bear the other name of the Pavilion,
Yusheitongzuo Xuan , "With Whom Shall I Sit?" Pavilion.

184

Delicate banisters stretch deep into the tranquil gardens; beyond willows vernal scenery spreads onto the horizon.

深院宇
小闌干
楊柳外無邊春色

拙政园曲廊
A winding veranda in Zhuozheng Yuan (the Humble Administrator's Garden)

留听阁正立面图
| Front elevation of Liuting Ge (the
Stay and Listen Pavilion)

留听阁平面图
| Floor plan of Liuting Ge
(the Stay and Listen Pavilion)

留听阁侧立面图
| Side elevation of Liuting Ge
(the Stay and Listen Pavilion)

The red roses swinging on a
day blue and bright;
Their shadows swaying on the
window with delight.

紅薇影轉晴窗畫

拙政园留听阁

Liuting Ge (the Stay and Listen Pavilion) in Zhuozheng Yuan
(the Humble Administrator's Garden)

塔影亭立面图
| Elevation of Taying Ting (the
Pagoda Reflection Pavilion)

塔影亭平面图
| Floor plan of Taying Ting (the
Pagoda Reflection Pavilion)

塔影亭俯视图
| Top view of Taying Ting (the
Pagoda Reflection Pavilion)

In front of the steps, a
riot of flowers grows sun
bright; under the bridge,
a ribbon of a stream
gurgles day and night.

階前花影亂
橋下水聲長

拙政园塔影亭

Taying Ting (the Pagoda Reflection Pavilion) in Zhuozheng
Yuan (the Humble Administrator's Garden)

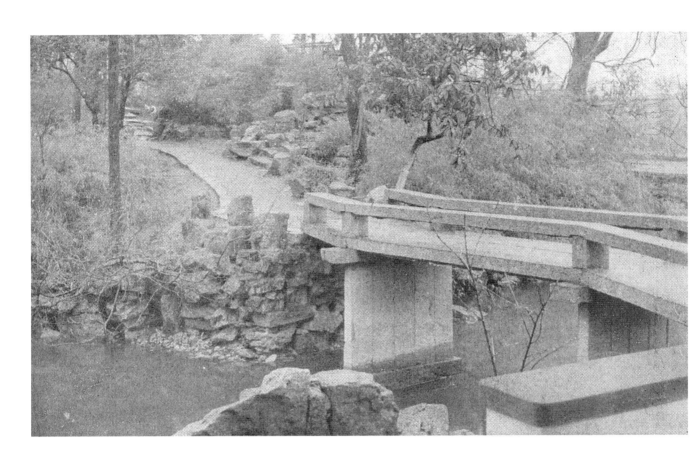

A trail snakes through bamboo wild and rank; lush and sweet grass flourishes on the pond's bank.

乱竹分幽径
芳草到横塘

拙政园三曲桥

Sanqu Qiao (the Three Fold Zigzag Bridge) in Zhuozheng Yuan (the Humble Administrator's Garden)

Flowers dance gracefully
on the ground;
with flecks of shadow
swirling around.

花影婆婆清畫永

拙政园远香堂踏跺

Step stones in front of Yuanxiang Tang (the Hall
of Distant Fragrance) in Zhuozheng Yuan (the
Humble Administrator's Garden)

Leaning pines break out
by the steps of stone;
In the shade of cliffs
withered moss is
overgrown.

拙政园远香堂前树根

Tree roots by Yuanxiang Tang (the Hall of Distant Fragrance) in
Zhuozheng Yuan (the Humble Administrator's Garden)

腰门正立面图
| Front elevation of Yaomen (side gate of the Garden)

腰门背立面图
| Back elevation of Yaomen (side gate of the Garden)

腰门平面图
| Floor plan of Yaomen (side gate of the Garden)

腰门横断面图
| Cross section of Yaomen (side gate of the Garden)

涵碧山房环境图
| Site plan of Hanbi Shanfang
(The Hanbi [Be imbued with the green] Mountain Villa)

绿荫及古木交柯前长廊正立面图
| Front elevation of Lüyin (the Green Shade Pavilion) and
the veranda in front of Gumujiaoke
(the Intertwined Old Trees)

I pen down my will of
homecoming on the wall:
That not even huge green
mountains can stall.

素壁写归来
青山遮不住

留园古木交柯前长廊

The veranda in front of Gumujiaoke (the Intertwined Old
Trees) in Liuyuan (the Lingering Garden)

古木交柯前长廊横断面图
| Cross section of the veranda in front of Gumujiaoke (the Intertwined Old Trees)

绿荫横断面图
| Cross section of Lüyin
(the Green Shade Pavilion)

The window is half ablaze with sun shining; the water sparkles but without any rippling.

半窗晴日水痕收

留园绿荫
Lüyin (the Green Shade Pavilion) in Liuyuan (the Lingering Garden)

明瑟楼二层平面及屋顶仰视图
| Floor plan and mirror reflection of ceiling plan, first floor of Mingse Lou (the Pellucid or The Pure Freshness Tower)

明瑟楼底层平面及上层仰视图
| Floor plan and mirror reflection of ceiling plan, ground floor of Mingse Lou (the Pellucid or The Pure Freshness Tower)

Myriad rails set each other off with their radiant vermilion. The setting sun shines the cottages and waterside pavilion.

朱闌聊掩映
夕陽低戶水當樓

留园明瑟楼及绿荫

Mingse Lou (the Pellucid or The Pure Freshness Tower) and Lüying (the Green Shade Pavilion) in Liuyuan (the Lingering Garden)

明瑟楼侧立面图
| Side elevation of Mingse Lou
(the Pellucid or The Pure Freshness Tower)

Freeze rises trees in
nature's calls leaves
desert trees of parasol.
All harbingers of
imminent fall.

涼風生玉宇
梧桐吹下新秋

留园明瑟楼

Mingse Lou (the Pellucid or The Pure Freshness Tower) in
Liuyuan (the Lingering Garden)

涵碧山房背立面图及明瑟楼正立面图
| Back elevation of Hanbi Shanfang (the Hanbi [Be imbued with
the green] Mountain Villa) and front elevation of Mingse Lou (the
Pellucid or The Pure Freshness Tower)

涵碧山房平面图
| Floor plan of Hanbi Shanfang
(the Hanbi [Be imbued with the green] Mountain Villa)

Leaning over the emerald
balustrade in fair autumn,
I enjoy the silvery moonshine
and the lotus blossom.

长爱碧阑干影
芙蓉秋水开时

留园涵碧山房

Hanbi Shanfang (the Hanbi [Be imbued with the green]
Mountain Villa) in Liuyuan (the Lingering Garden)

涵碧山房正立面图
| Front elevation of Hanbi Shanfang (the Hanbi [Be imbued with
the green] Mountain Villa)

涵碧山房横断面图
| Cross section of Hanbi Shanfang
(the Hanbi [Be imbued with the green] Mountain Villa)

Ornate rails skirting
exquisite towers.

曲折画阑
玲珑楼阁

留园涵碧山房及明瑟楼

Hanbi Shanfang (the Hanbi [Be imbued with the green]
Mountain Villa) and Mingse Lou (the Pellucid or The Pure
Freshness Tower) in Liuyuan (the Lingering Garden)

闻木樨香轩环境图
| Site plan of Wenmuxixiang Xuan
(the Osmanthus Fragrance Pavilion)

1. 闻木樨香轩 | Wenmuxixiang Xuan
2. 可亭 | Keting
3. 凉台 | Liangtai
4. 涵碧山房 | Hanbi Shanfang
5. 明瑟楼 | Mingse Lou

A graceful bower towers
over terraced trails.
Caressed by sentient
flowers and hugged by
love-sick rails

留园凉台

Liangtai (Terrace at the north of Hanbi Shanfang [The Hanbi
(Be imbued with the green) Mountain Villa]) in Liuyuan (the
Lingering Garden)

闻木樨香轩正立面图
| Front elevation of Wenmuxixiang Xuan
(the Osmanthus Fragrance Pavilion)

闻木樨香轩屋顶仰视及俯视图
| Mirror reflection of ceiling plan and roof plan of
Wenmuxixiang Xuan (the Osmanthus Fragrance Pavilion)

闻木樨香轩平面图
| Floor plan of Wenmuxixiang Xuan
(the Osmanthus Fragrance Pavilion)

The beauty of the stream
ringed hillock is beyond
compare.
With its rain cleaned grass,
radiant sunset and fresh air.

谿山無限好
雨餘芳草斜陽

留园闻木樨香轩
Wenmuxixiang Xuan (the Osmanthus Fragrance Pavilion) in
Liuyuan (the Lingering Garden)

水阁平面图
| Floor plan of Shuige

水阁正立面图
| Front elevation of Shuige

水阁横断面图
| Cross section of Shuige

Flimsy mist wafting among the trees at dusk: Osmanthus rollicking in the autumn air brisk.

暝烟带树
满庭秋色木樨花

留园闻木樨香轩曲廊

Winding veranda at Wenmuxixiang Xuan (the Osmanthus Fragrance Pavilion) in Liuyuan (the Lingering Garden)

亦不二亭正立面图
| Front elevation of Yibu'er Ting

亦不二亭平面图
| Floor plan of Yibu'er Ting

亦不二亭横断面图
| Cross section of Yibu'er Ting

Along the long winding corridor I found myself strolling, while the yard is quiet and the sun is still lingering.

留园闻木樨香轩曲廊
Winding veranda at Wenmuxixiang Xuan (the Osmanthus Fragrance Pavilion) in Liuyuan (the Lingering Garden)

可亭环境图
| Site plan of Keting (the Passable Pavilion)

1. 闻木樨香轩 | Wenmuxixiang Xuan
2. 可亭 | Keting
3. 远翠阁（自在处）| Yuancui Ge (Zizaichu)
4. 汲古得绠处 | Jigudegengchu
5. 小蓬莱 | Xiao Penglai

可亭断面图
| Section of Keting (the Passable Pavilion)

可亭立面图
| Elevation of Keting
  (the Passable Pavilion)

可亭平面及屋顶仰视图
| Floor and ceiling plan of Keting (the Passable Pavilion)

The dainty to tower and
the painted pavilion,
I air off to charm the
spring filled garden.

留园自明瑟楼北望可亭

Keting (the Passable Pavilion) in Liuyuan (the Lingering Garden),
viewed from Mingse Lou (the Pellucid or The Pure Freshness
Tower)

五峰仙馆环境图
| Site plan of Wufengxian Guan
(the Celestial Hall of Five Peaks)

1. 远翠阁（自在处）| Yuancui Ge (Zizaichu)
2. 汲古得绠处 | Jigudegengchu
3. 清风池馆 | Qingfengchi Guan
4. 五峰仙馆（楠木厅）| Wufengxian Guan

A tower bathed in spring.

留园自五峰仙馆望远翠阁

Yuancui Ge (the Distant Green Tower) in Liuyuan (the Lingering
Garden), viewed from Wufengxian Guan (the Celestial Hall of
Five Peaks)

远翠阁二层平面及屋顶仰视图
| Floor plan and mirror reflection of ceiling plan
(first floor) of Yuancui Ge (the Distant Green Tower)

远翠阁底层平面图
| Floor plan (ground floor) of Yuancui Ge (the
Distant Green Tower)

远翠阁横断面图
| Cross section of Yuancui Ge (the Distant Green Tower)

Bowers and towers are decked with
charm profound.
Setting tumi flowers blooming all
over the ground.
And sending fluffy catkins flying
about and around.

留园自凉台东北望远翠阁及汲古得绠处等
Yuancui Ge (the Distant Green Tower) and Jigudegengchu (the Study
of Enlightenment) in Liuyuan (the Lingering Garden), viewed from
Liangtai (Terrace at the north of Hanbi Shanfang [The Hanbi (Be
imbued with the green) Mountain Villa])

远翠阁侧立面图
| Side elevation of Yuancui Ge
(the Distant Green Tower)

远翠阁正立面图
| Front elevation of Yuancui Ge
(the Distant Green Tower)

Fainty flowers nestling
by the cute tower.

留园远翠阁
Yuancui Ge (the Distant Green Tower) in Liuyuan (the
Lingering Garden)

濠濮亭正立面图
| Front elevation of Haopu Ting
　(the Haopu Pavilion)

濠濮亭平面图
| Floor plan of Haopu Ting
　(the Haopu Pavilion)

A pavilion perching
over steps.

留园濠濮亭
Haopu Ting (the Haopu Pavilion) in Liuyuan (the
Lingering Garden)

1. 曲溪楼｜Quxi Lou
2. 西楼｜Xilou
3. 清风池馆｜Qingfengchi Guan

曲溪楼、西楼二层平面图
| Floor plan of first floor of Quxi Lou (the Winding Stream Tower) and Xilou (Western Tower)

曲溪楼、西楼及清风池馆底层平面图
| Floor plan of ground floor of Quxi Lou (the Winding Stream Tower), Xilou (Western Tower) and Qingfengchi Guan (the Refreshing Breeze Pavilion by the Lake)

A marble house with a jade-like hall.

瓊樓玉宇

留园曲溪楼、西楼及清风池馆

From right to left: Quxi Lou (the Winding Stream Tower), Xilou (Western Tower) and Qingfengchi Guan (the Refreshing Breeze Pavilion by the Lake) in Liuyuan (the Lingering Garden)

清风池馆横断面图
| Cross section of Qingfengchi Guan
(the Refreshing Breeze Pavilion by the Lake)

曲溪楼、西楼及清风池馆正立面图
| Front elevation of Quxi Lou (the Winding Stream Tower), Xilou (Western Tower) and
Qingfengchi Guan (the Refreshing Breeze Pavilion by the Lake)

Wooden slippers echoing
from the depth of the
long corridor; lush trees
frolicking with their shade
in the noon's splendor.

留园曲溪楼

Quxi Lou (the Winding Stream Tower) in Liuyuan (the
Lingering Garden)

西楼横断面图
| Cross section of Xilou (Western Tower)

曲溪楼横断面图
| Cross section of Quxi Lou (the Winding Stream Tower)

The pale shadow of sun bright blossoms waving on the window.

瑣愡淡、花影薄

留园西楼
Xilou (Western Tower) in Liuyuan (the Lingering Garden)

玉階小立
十分竹瘦松堅

Slim bamboo and
sturdy pine stand by
the steps of jade nice
and fine.

留园五峰仙馆前
Front of Wufengxian Guan (the Celestial Hall of Five Peaks)
in Liuyuan (the Lingering Garden)

五峰仙馆背立面图
| Back elevation of Wufengxian Guan
(the Celestial Hall of Five Peaks)

五峰仙馆平面图
| Floor plan of Wufengxian Guan
(the Celestial Hall of Five Peaks)

Spring sprayed art
gallery.

留园五峰仙馆内部

Interior of Wufengxian Guan (the Celestial Hall of Five
Peaks) in Liuyuan (the Lingering Garden)

五峰仙馆正立面图
| Front elevation of Wufengxian Guan
(the Celestial Hall of Five Peaks)

五峰仙馆横断面图
| Cross section of Wufengxian Guan
(the Celestial Hall of Five Peaks)

五峰仙馆纵断面图
| Longitudinal section of Wufengxian Guan
(the Celestial Hall of Five Peaks)

sparse bamboo shedding
slender shadows
jaged rocks scraping the
sky blue and helen.

萧疏竹影
乱石穿空

留园五峰仙馆西侧

West side of Wufengxian Guan (the Celestial Hall of Five Peaks) in
Liuyuan (the Lingering Garden)

五峰仙馆侧立面图
| Side elevation of Wufengxian Guan
(the Celestial Hall of Five Peaks)

Jade green bamboo and
sweet-smelling moss
in the depth of the yard
grow lush with gloss.

竹色苔香小院深

留园五峰仙馆东侧小院

Small court yard at the east side of Wufengxian Guan (the
Celestial Hall of Five Peaks) in Liuyuan (the Lingering Garden)

汲古得绠处横断面图
| Cross section of Jigudegengchu
(the Study of Enlightenment)

汲古得绠处平面图
| Floor plan of Jigudegengchu
(the Study of Enlightenment)

汲古得绠处正立面图
| Front elevation of Jigudegengchu
(the Study of Enlightenment)

轻阴小庭院
欲晴天雨雨还晴

Shreds of clouds sail over
the small garden,
Shedding fitful drizzle in
shafts of light of heaven.

留园汲古得绠处

Jigudegengchu (the Study of Enlightenment) in Liuyuan (the
Lingering Garden)

还我读书处横断面图
| Cross section of Huanwodushuchu
 (the Return-to-Read Study)

还我读书处正立面图
| Front elevation of Huanwodushuchu
 (the Return-to-Read Study)

还我读书处二层平面图
| First floor plan of Huanwodushuchu
 (the Return-to-Read Study)

还我读书处底层平面图
| Ground floor plan of Huanwodushuchu
 (the Return-to-Read Study)

Moonlight creeping
through the window of
an unlit attic.

留园还我读书处
Huanwodushuchu (the Return-to-Read Study)
in Liuyuan (the Lingering Garden)

Autumn bamboo serenading
by the window.

竹
送
秋
聲
到
小
牕

留园揖峰轩内

Interior of Yifeng Xuan (the Worshipping Stone Pavilion)
in Liuyuan (the Lingering Garden)

The serene yard like a maze is deftly laid, And skirted with delicacy by carved balustrade.

閒院深迷
雕欄巧護

留园揖峰轩曲廊
Winding veranda at Yifeng Xuan (the Worshipping Stone Pavilion) in Liuyuan (the Lingering Garden)

揖峰轩

揖峰轩环境图
| Site plan of Yifeng Xuan
(the Worshipping Stone Pavilion)

半窗晴翠

留园揖峰轩前小景
Scene in front of Yifeng Xuan (the Worshipping Stone
Pavilion) in Liuyuan (the Lingering Garden)

揖峰轩横断面图
| Cross section of Yifeng Xuan
(the Worshipping Stone Pavilion)

揖峰轩正立面图
| Front elevation of Yifeng Xuan
(the Worshipping Stone Pavilion)

Shrouded in the groves deep,
Nestled in the hill steep,
A homestead is half-veiled
in shades of green.
And overgrown with palm
battered by showers of rain.

留园揖峰轩前小院

Courtyard in front of Yifeng Xuan (the Worshipping Stone Pavilion) in
Liuyuan (the Lingering Garden)

活泼泼地正立面图
| Front elevation of Huopopodi
(the Place of Liveliness)

活泼泼地横断面图
| Cross section of Huopopodi
(the Place of Liveliness)

The sun shines bright.
The breeze caresses light.
The day of spring lingers
longer, and stays sheltel
the night.

日丽风和春昼长

留园揖峰轩前
Front of Yifeng Xuan (the Worshipping Stone Pavilion)
in Liuyuan (the Lingering Garden)

活泼泼地环境图
| Site plan of Huopopodi
 (the Place of Liveliness)

1. 活泼泼地 | Huopopodi

活泼泼地平面图
| Floor plan of Huopopodi
 (the Place of Liveliness)

活泼泼地侧立面图
| Side elevation of Huopopodi
 (the Place of Liveliness)

Beyond the flaming flowers
ripples on vernal brook
spreading;
Inside the white washed
walls willow and osmanthus
blooming.

春水綠波花影外
粉牆丹桂柳蔭中

留园活泼泼地
Huopopodi (the Place of Liveliness) in Liuyuan (the
Lingering Garden)

林泉耆硕之馆正立面图
| Front elevation of Linquanqishuozhi Guan
(the Old Hermit Scholars' Hall)

林泉耆硕之馆侧立面图
| Side elevation of Linquanqishuozhi Guan
(the Old Hermit Scholars' Hall)

林泉耆硕之馆平面图
| Floor plan of Linquanqishuozhi Guan
(the Old Hermit Scholars' Hall)

Flower-scented grand hall.

堂深花气满

留园林泉耆硕之馆内部

Interior of Linquanqishuozhi Guan (the Old Hermit Scholars' Hall) in
Liuyuan (the Lingering Garden)

林泉耆硕之馆纵断面图
| Longitudinal section of Linquanqishuozhi Guan (the
Old Hermit Scholars' Hall)

林泉耆硕之馆及冠云楼横断面图
| Cross section of Linquanqishuozhi Guan (the Old Hermit Scholars' Hall)
and Guanyun Lou (the Cloud-Capped Tower)

From lush trees stands out
the jade-green house.
Hugged by antique walls
coated with shiny brown
moss. Isn't it Eden in the
world mundane?
One can't but feel at a loss.

留园林泉耆硕之馆前

Front of Linquanqishuozhi Guan (the Old Hermit Scholars' Hall) in
Liuyuan (the Lingering Garden)

1. 冠云楼 | Guanyun Lou
2. 冠云亭 | Guanyun Ting
3. 仁云庵 | Zhuyun'an
4. 冠云台 | Guanyun Tai

冠云楼环境图
| Site plan of Guanyun Lou
  (the Cloud-Capped Tower)

冠云楼横断面图
| Cross section of Guanyun Lou
  (the Cloud-Capped Tower)

The courtyard lies
tranquil under azure
sky; into cold air shoot
up two giant rocks
nearby.

留园冠云峰
Guanyun Feng (the Cloud-Capped Peak) in Liuyuan (the
Lingering Garden)

冠云楼屋顶仰视图
| Ceiling plan of Guanyun Lou
  (the Cloud-Capped Tower)

冠云楼二层平面图
| First floor plan of Guanyun Lou
  (the Cloud-Capped Tower)

冠云楼底层平面图
| Ground floor plan of Guanyun Lou
  (the Cloud-Capped Tower)

冠云楼正立面图
| Front elevation of Guanyun Lou
  (the Cloud-Capped Tower)

Lail-rimmed tortuous
veranda prostrate
afore the emerald tower.

留园冠云楼前曲廊
Winding veranda in front of Guanyun Lou (the Cloud-Capped
Tower) in Liuyuan (the Lingering Garden)

仁云庵正面图
| Front elevation of Zhuyun'an

仁云庵平面图
| Floor plan of Zhuyun'an

Pacing along the petal-paved
sprawling pathway;
Touched by the gaudy colors
on sentient display.

客行花径曲
幾多綠意紅情

留园冠云楼前曲廊

Winding veranda in front of Guanyun Lou (the Cloud-
Capped Tower) in Liuyuan (the Lingering Garden)

仁云庵侧立面图
| Side elevation of Zhuyun'an

仁云庵横断面图
| Cross section of Zhuyun'an

The corridor of the yard
is winding around;
Sun lit fair flowers
everywhere abound.

小院迴廊
暖日明花柳

留园曲廊

A winding veranda in Liuyuan (the Lingering Garden)

冠云亭正立面图
| Front elevation of Guanyun Ting
(the Cloud-Capped Pavilion)

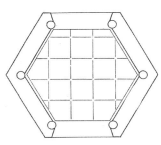

冠云亭平面图
| Floor plan of Guanyun Ting
(the Cloud-Capped Pavilion)

Spring prevails in the park's
every corner,
Vanquishing the barren and
bleak winter.

寒却园林春已透

留园冠云亭

Guanyun Ting (the Cloud-Capped Pavilion) in Liuyuan (the
Lingering Garden)

东园一角亭环境图

| Site plan of a pavilion at the corner of eastern section

东园一角亭平面及屋顶仰视图

| Floor and ceiling plan of a pavilion at the
corner of eastern section

东园一角亭立面图

| Elevation of a pavilion at the corner of eastern section

Graceful posture.

留园东园一角亭

A pavilion at the corner of east section of Liuyuan (the
Lingering Garden)

A thatch of yellow
day lily.
A bunch of dainty
bamboo.
A patch of plantain.

一叢萱草
幾竿修竹
數葉芭蕉

留园瑞云峰

Ruiyun Feng (the Auspicious Cloud Peak) in Liuyuan (the
Lingering Garden)

Delicate beauty.

留园岫云峰

Xiuyun Feng (the Mountainous Cloud Peak) in
Liuyuan (the Lingering Garden)

佳晴喜雨快雪之亭及冠云台横断面图
| Cross section of Jiaqingxiyukuaixuezhi Ting
(the Good-For-Farming Pavilion) and Guanyun Tai
(the Cloud-Capped Terrace)

佳晴喜雨快雪之亭正立面图
| Front elevation of Jiaqingxiyukuaixuezhi Ting
(the Good-For-Farming Pavilion)

佳晴喜雨快雪之亭平面图
| Floor plan of Jiaqingxiyukuaixuezhi Ting
 (the Good-For-Farming Pavilion)

留园佳晴喜雨快雪之亭槅扇

Partition Frames in Jiaqingxiyukuaixuezhi Ting (the Good-For-
Farming Pavilion) in Liuyuan (the Lingering Garden)

Misty wild woodland revoking no end of imagination.

古木蒼煙無限意

留园至乐亭

Zhile Ting (the Delightful Pavilion) in
Liuyuan (the Lingering Garden)

至乐亭正立面图
| Front elevation of Zhile Ting
(the Delightful Pavilion)

至乐亭及舒啸亭环境图
| Site plan of Zhile Ting (the Delightful Pavilion) and Shuxiao Ting (the Free Roaring Pavilion）

1. 至乐亭 | Zhile Ting
2. 舒啸亭 | Shuxiao Ting
3. 活泼泼地 | Huopopodi

至乐亭平面图
| Floor plan of Zhile Ting (the Delightful Pavilion)

至乐亭横断面图
| Cross section of Zhile Ting (the Delightful Pavilion)

舒啸亭横断面图
| Cross section of Shuxiao Ting
(the Free Roaring Pavilion)

舒啸亭立面图
| Elevation of Shuxiao Ting
(the Free Roaring Pavilion)

舒啸亭平面图
| Floor plan of Shuxiao Ting
(the Free Roaring Pavilion

Weary of flying, birds
flit back to the nests;
Languid of hovering,
clouds hasten home
around the crests.

留园舒啸亭

Shuxiao Ting (the Free Roaring Pavilion) in Liuyuan
(the Lingering Garden)

274

Spring follows where
the heart goes.

留园西部云墙

Yunqiang (the Undulating Wall) in western section of
Liuyuan (the Lingering Garden)

Breeze brushed branches of
willow in spring,
Before the bower frivolously
sway and swing.

風梳萬縷亭前柳

留园西部曲廊

A winding veranda in western section of Liuyuan (the
Lingering Garden)

陈列馆环境图（又一村）
| Site plan of Exhitibion Hall (Youyicun)

陈列馆平面图
| Floor plan of Exhibition Hall

The garden of flowers
and grass, sweet and
fair, graced now and
then by pale moonlight
and gentle air.

留园新建陈列馆
New built Exhibition Hall in Liuyuan (the Lingering
Garden)

Spring sprinkled
pear park.

春在梨花院

狮子林立雪堂望院中

Courtyard of Lixue Tang (the Standing-in-Snow Hall) in
Shizilin (the Lion Forest Garden)

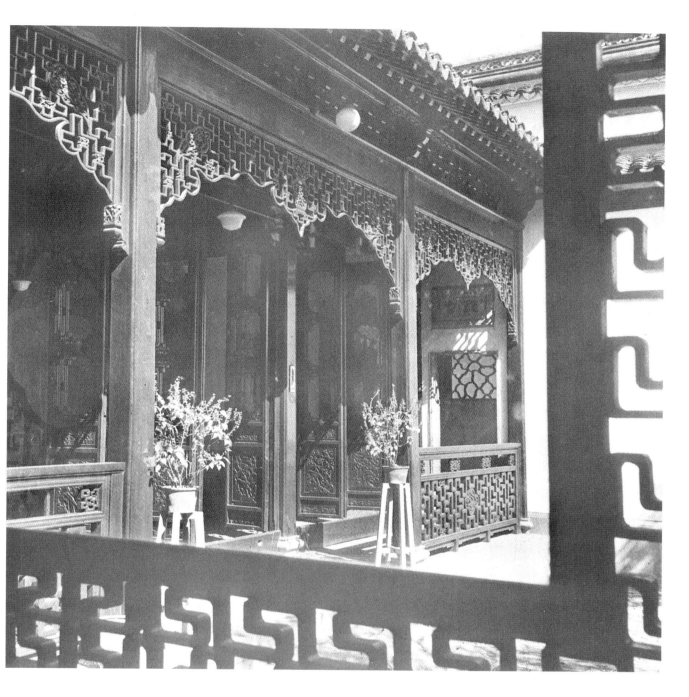

To wine and dine
guests at the
scented hall of orchid.

蘭堂有酒留佳客

狮子林立雪堂望燕誉堂

Yanyu Tang (the Hall of Peace and Happiness) in
Shizilin (the Lion Forest Garden), viewed from
Lixue Tang (the Standing-in-Snow Hall)

During the day the
sun shines on the shut
window, toward the eve
the screen still hangs
quiet and low.

昼永瑣揔閒
日遅簾幕静

狮子林小方厅后院
Backyard of Xiaofang Ting (the Small Square Hall) in
Shizilin (the Lion Forest Garden)

日暮深院静
牡丹红药时光

狮子林牡丹台

A raised peony flower bed in Shizilin (the Lion Forest Garden)

In search of serene beauty.

狮子林探幽门

Tanyou Men (Places of Repose Sought) in Shizilin
(the Lion Forest Garden)

曲亭深院
美景良辰

狮子林修竹阁

Xiuzhu Ge (the Bamboo Pavilion) in Shizilin (the Lion
Forest Garden)

The fig withered and the moss worn; fondle the steep rocks, if you care, only to find myriad peaks still shone with the light of moon.

狮子林指柏轩前

Front of Zhibai Xuan (the Pointing at Cypress Hall) in Shizilin (the Lion Forest Garden)

試向溪邊問　春從何處來

Where the spring?
Back to the stream
I turn to enquire!

狮子林扇面亭

Shanmian Ting (the Fan Pavilion) in Shizilin (the Lion
Forest Garden)

The stream tumbling at
the height of spring,
over the verdant meadow
burgeoning sprigs swing,
and on the airy bower
magic lights fling.

修水濃春
新條漢綠
翠光交映盧亭

狮子林湖心亭
Huxin Ting (the Mid-Lake Pavilion) in Shizilin (the Lion Forest
Garden)

人去月侵廊
花下凌波入夢

狮子林曲廊
A winding veranda in Shizilin (the Lion Forest Garden)

The mild sun of spring
sprinkles its light around;
The pale shade of pines
sprawls the yard ground.

狮子林古五松园

Guwusong Yuan (the Garden of Five Age-old Pines) in
Shizilin (the Lion Forest Garden)

水底看山影
依庸千岩萬岫

Mirror underwater are
hills, ridge upon ridge,
Laliuz the eve with
their untimed images,
edge after edge.

狮子林假山
Rockeries in Shizilin (the Lion Forest Garden)

Crashed aground
from Leaven a bluish
mount: whose divine
hands hacked it out?

天峰飛墮地
翠岩誰削

狮子林假山

Rockeries in Shizilin (the Lion Forest Garden)

The sturdy pines snuggling by the slim and supple bamboo; the gray rocks cloaked with moss, green or blue.

青松瘦竹
白石蒼苔

狮子林假山
Rockeries in Shizilin (the Lion Forest Garden)

A strip of water,
crystal and green,
flanked by rocks,
steep and stern.

狮子林石洞

A cavern in Shizilin (the Lion Forest Garden)

Field after field
stretching far and wide,
A stream's fresh green
ripples flowing astride.

田田多少
一溪新綠漲晴波

芝圃石桥

A stone bridge in Yipu (the Garden of Cultivation)

涓
涓
流
水
細
侵
階

艺圃小桥

A pedestrian stone bridge in Yipu (the Garden of Cultivation)

Over the pond, around the bower and flower bed, spring morn lingers with light spread, darkening the green and paling the red.

池閣長春曉
園林綠晴紅稀

环秀山庄一角

A scenery spot in Huanxiu Shanzhuang (the Mountain Villa with Embracing Beauty)

The tall trees try
with the sunset glow;
Along the dim dale
swirling winds blow.

高林弄残照
幽壑舞迴风

环秀山庄假山

Rockeries in Huanxiu Shanzhuang (the Mountain Villa with
Embracing Beauty)

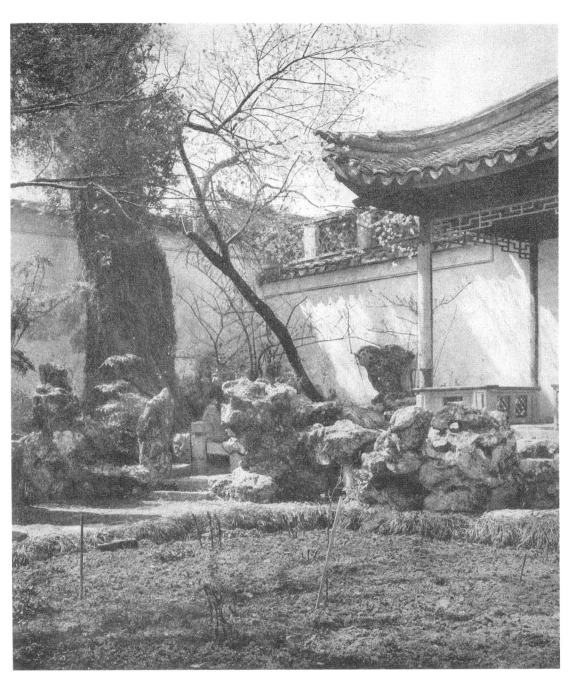

Delicate flowers in the
deep and quiet yard
grow through wispy
mist sun rays warm the
vine below.

小花深院静
日烘芳烛下藤萝

网师园小景
A scenery spot in Wangshi Yuan (the Master-of-Nets Garden)

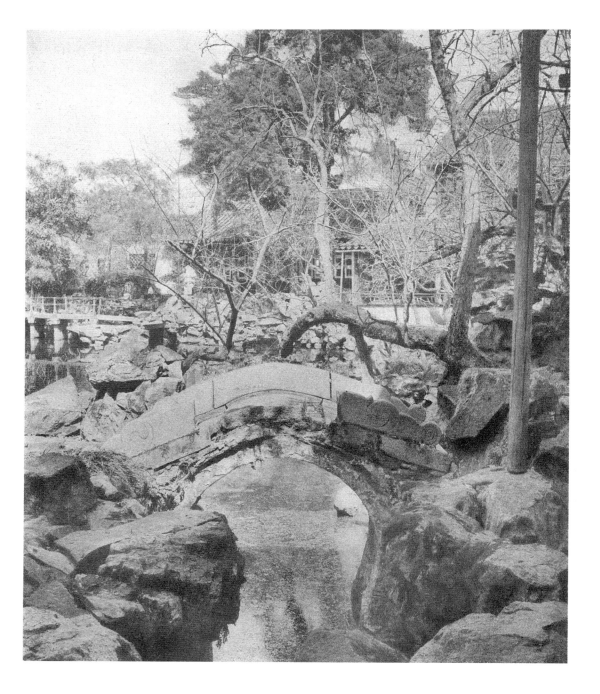

Sending for the Moon fairy
to shed her pearly light:
To turn the garden into a
pond of silvery white.

唤个月儿来
清光更多
只放冰壶一色

网师园小石桥（即"引静桥"）

A small pedestrian arch bridge in Wangshi Yuan (the Master-of-Nets
Garden) (This bridge is called "Yinjing Qiao (The Leading to Quietude
Bridge)" now.)

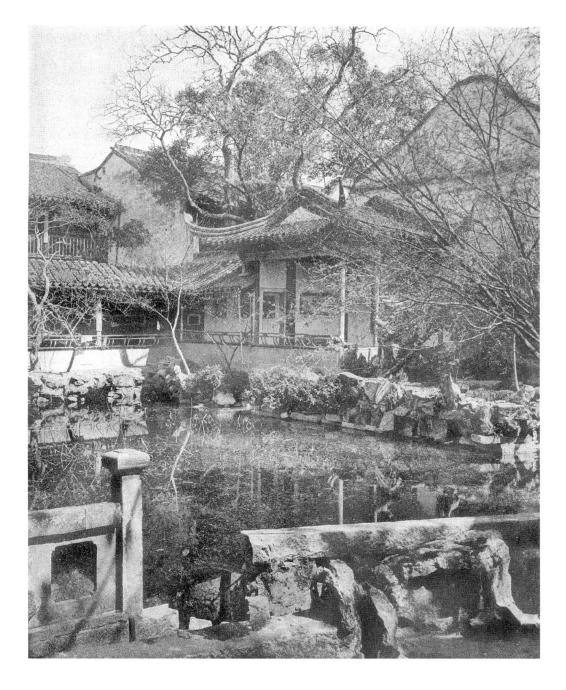

Spring delights in her stay within the jade rails; swallows sing over a maze of flowery trails.

网师园东部一角

A scenery spot in the eastern section of Wangshi Yuan (the Master-of-Nets Garden)

Beyond the winding rails,
far into the horizon: heaven
in water, water in heaven.

网师园长廊水亭（即"月到风来亭"）

A pavilion over the water along with roofed walkway in Wangshi Yuan
(the Master-of-Nets Garden) (This pavilion is called " Yuedaofenglai
Ting (The Moon Comes With Breeze Pavilion)" now.)

流水花間
曲榭芳亭初埽

With water flowing
and flowers blooming
all around.
The newly
swept pavilion is even
more enchanting.

网师园水亭（即"月到风来亭"）

A pavilion over the water in Wangshi Yuan (the Master-of-Nets
Garden) (This pavilion is called " Yuedaofenglai Ting (The
Moon Comes With Breeze Pavilion)" now.)

There lies a crystal clear
and jade like pond;
With wispy grass in
spring breeze swaying
around.

一鏡無塵
細草靜搖春碧

网师园西北部

A north west part of Wangshi Yuan (the Master-of-
Nets Garden)

A window embroidered
with flower shadow.

花影透綺窗

怡园复廊漏窗

Lattice window in the double-corridor of Yiyuan (the Garden
of Pleasance)

305

Patches of greenish moss
clings to the face of a grey
crag; the trail of a yard
winds along a hedge loose
and zigzag.

怡园拜石轩前

Front of Baishi Xuan (Rock Worshipping Pavilion) in
Yiyuan (the Garden of Pleasance)

憑闌看落日
斷虹斜界雨初晴

I watch by the rail
the rain-washed
sunset flow.
And thrill at the
sky-striding broken
rainbow.

怡园藕香榭
Ouxiang Xie (Lotus Scent Studio) in Yiyuan
(the Garden of Pleasance)

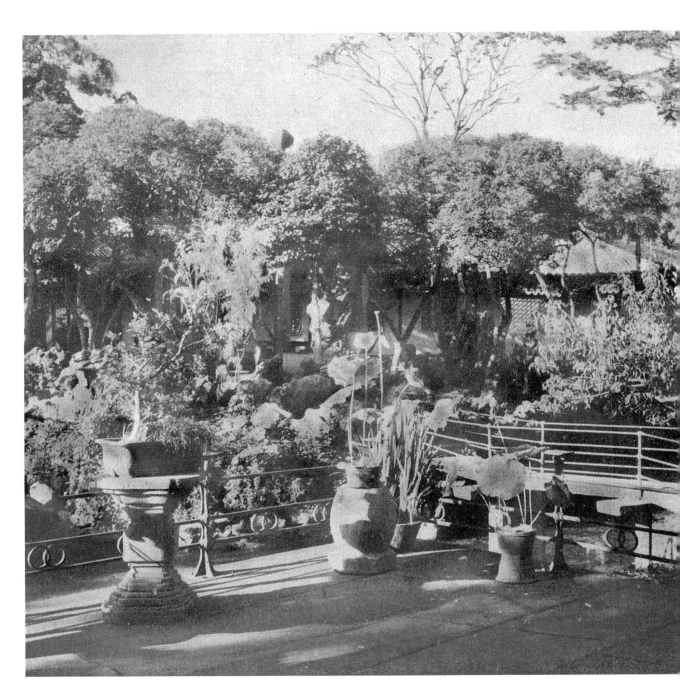

Enfolding their dainty
and fresh green:
The newly sprung lotuses
enliven the scene.

小小新荷
點破清光景趣多

怡园藕香榭前

Front of Ouxiang Xie (Lotus Scent Studio) in
Yiyuan (the Garden of Pleasance)

绿往穿花

留园涵碧山房前铺地

Patterned pavement in front of Hanbi Shanfang (the Hanbi
[Be imbued with the green] Mountain Villa) in Liuyuan (the
Lingering Garden)

Human shadows
shuffling in the
radiance of blossoms.

花光人影

怡园镜中小沧浪

Xiaocanglang (the Small Canglang) in Yiyuan (the Garden
of Pleasance), reflected in a mirror.

Shower-cleansed, the fall
air feels fresh and nice;
Mist-engulfed, the aged
trees evoke emotional
sighs.

玉宇洗清秋
古木蒼烟無限意

怡园旱船

The Boat-Like Pavilion in Yiyuan (the Garden of
Pleasance)

In the fresh bamboo
grove, tender green
sprigs all sway;
In the grass-hugged
path, verdant moss
sprawls all the way.

新篁嫩
搖碧
玉
芳徑綠苔
生

怡园岁寒草庐前

Front of Suihan Caolu (Evergreen Thatched Cottage) in Yiyuan (the
Garden of Pleasance)

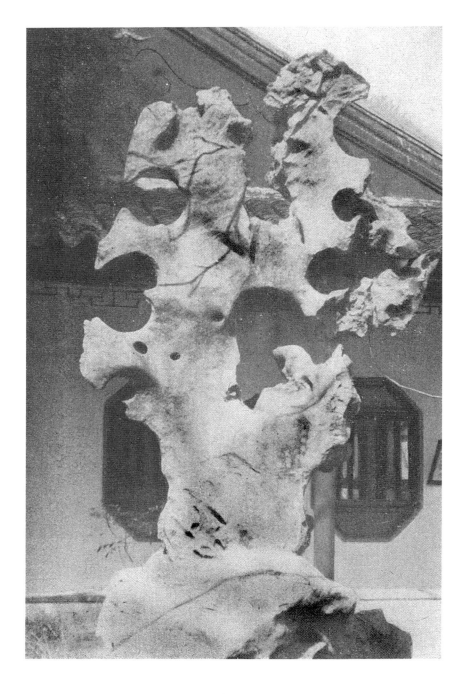

Lake rocks of
Yiyuan Garden.

怡园湖石

A limestone in Yiyuan (the Garden of Pleasance)

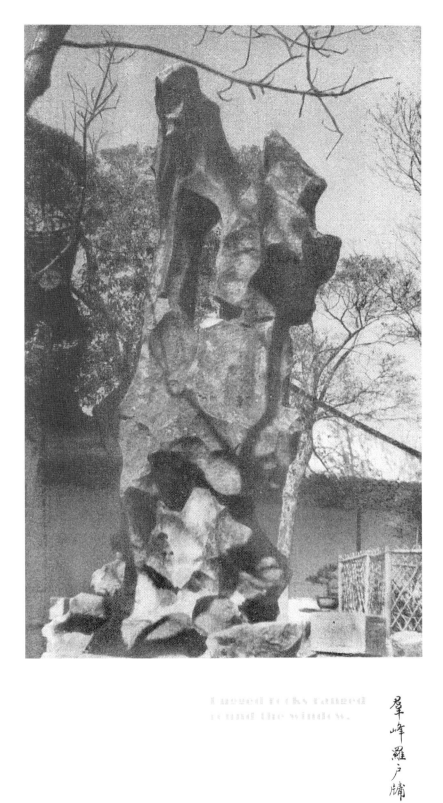

群峰羅戶牖

怡园湖石

A limestone in Yiyuan (the Garden of Pleasance)

Through the florid drapes up rolled, a flock of swallows are found back home, in the dappled shade of apricot grove.

杏花疏影裏
畫簾低捲燕遄來

西白塔子巷李氏园

Lishi Yuan (Li's Family Garden) in Xibaitazi Xiang (White Pagoda Alley)

The shadow of flowers
flashed on the wall,
seems like the strokes
of a fair girl.

滿身花影倩人扶

西白塔子巷李氏园
Lishi Yuan (Li's Family Garden) in Xibaitazi
Xiang (White Pagoda Alley)

317

Lushed Yard.

西白塔子巷李氏园

Lishi Yuan (Li`s Family Garden) in Xibaitazi Xiang
(White Pagoda Alley)

洞府藏幽

西白塔子巷李氏园
Lishi Yuan (Li's Family Garden) in Xibaitazi Xiang (White Pagoda Alley)

Spring graces the blossom shaded waterside bower.

芳草园一角
Fangcao Yuan (Fragrant Grass Garden)

柳上斜陽紅萬縷
烘人滿院荷香

The twilight turns
the tops of willow
into red radiance;
the lotus of the
garden sends off
whiffs of fragrance.

景德路慕家花园一角
Mu's Family Garden on Jingde Road

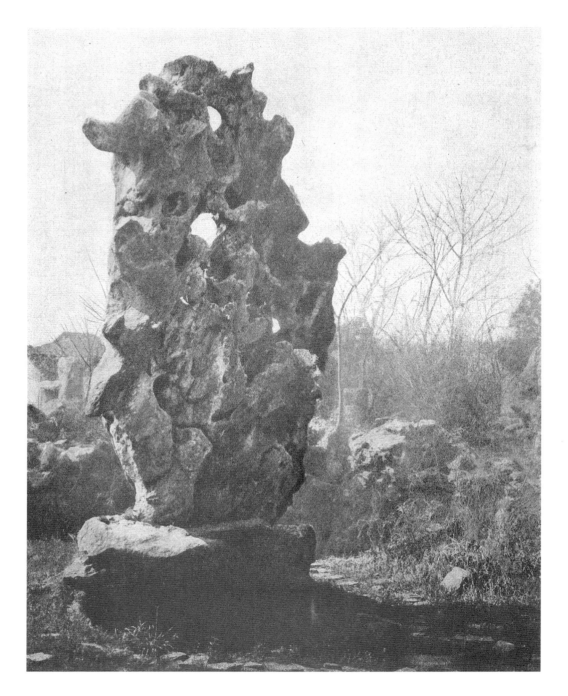

The steep cliffs scrape
massive clouds;
The jade peaks cap
the mounts proud.

峭壁重霄
奇峰献玉

带城桥江苏师范学院附属女子中学瑞云峰

Ruiyun Feng (the Auspicious Cloud Peak) located in the Girl's Secondary
School Associated to Jiangsu Normal College at Daichengqiao

燕語鶯塘小院幽
春色三分休

韩家巷鹤园一角
Heyuan (the Crane Garden) at Hanjia Xiang (Han's Family Alley)

Bewitched by the spring,
the twilight on willow
branches showers called
by the nature,
the yard yields all
seasonal flowers.

新枝媚斜日
小園自有四時花

醋库巷柴氏园

Chaishi Yuan (Chai's Garden) at Cuku Xiang

铁瓶巷颐宅花厅

Huating (Flower Hall) in Gu's House at Tieping Xiang

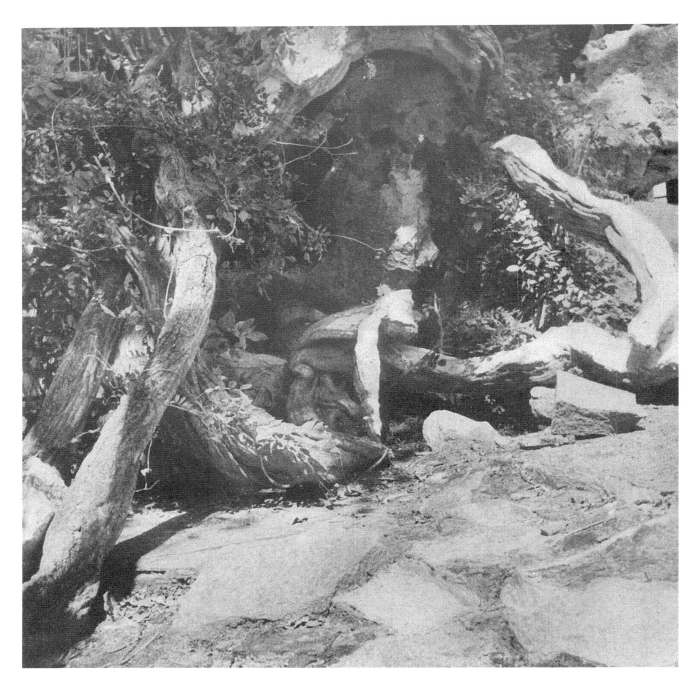

As the plum blooms,
the pond overflows;
Under the rainbow,
the moss grows.

梅風池漲
虹雨苔滋

惠荫园紫藤
Chinese Wisteria in Huiyin Yuan

喬木驚初囀
深院燕交飛

西百花巷程氏园

Cheng's Garden in Xibaihua Xiang

Through the green moss
wades a trodden trail;
Around the serene yard
winds a carved rail.

幽徑破苔痕
雕玉闌干深院靜

西百花巷程氏園花厅

Huating (Flower Hall) in Cheng's Garden in
Xibaihua Xiang

The sun shines bright
and long;
The jade green leaves
glisten off and on;
A darting cricle chants
a liquid song.

紅日長
綠烟晴
流鶯三兩聲

沧浪亭前可园一角

A corner of Keyuan (the Passable Garden) in front of the Garden of
Canglang Ting (the Canglang Pavilion)

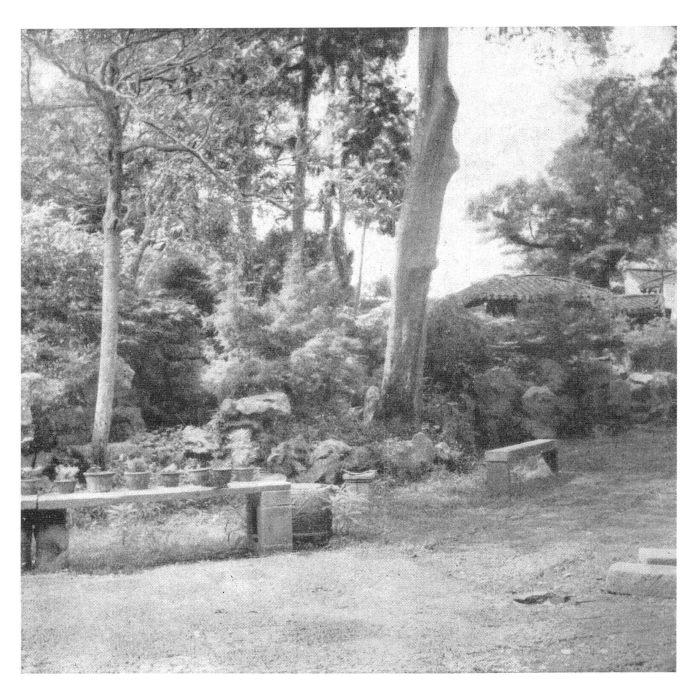

Sparse here and dense
there the age old trees
grow; through the ceiling
mist the sun blazes the
vine below.

古林疏又密
日烘芳炷下蘿藤

耦园花厅前一角

A corner in the front of Huating (Flower Hall) in
Ouyuan (the Couple's Garden Retreat)

A tall lotus hall stands
over a pond;
with green leaves and
red flowers threaded.

耦园东部荷花厅

Hehua Ting (Lotus Hall) in the east part of Ouyuan (the
Couple's Garden Retreat)

Sweet scent of osmanthus
suffusing the yard.

耦园西部藏书楼

The Library Tower in the west part of Ouyuan (the Couple's
Garden Retreat)

full-swing swing
feeding the idle.

耦园西部

West part of Ouyuan (the Couple's Garden Retreat)

Into the house wafts floral
fragrance of the night.
With bracing breeze and
bright moonlight, isn't it
the best time for delight.

曲房花氣靄
清風明月好時光

耦园西部

West part of Ouyuan (the Couple's Garden Retreat)

耦园西部曲廊

A winding veranda in the west part of Ouyuan (the Couple's
Garden Retreat)

Not any sound,
Daytime lingers
around, in the yard
no rambler is found.

人静静
日迟迟
深院断无人到

耦园西部小斋

A small house in the west part of Ouyuan (the Couple's Garden Retreat)

林霏散浮暝
水光月色兩相東

戒幢律寺西园水漏窗
Lattice window over the water in Jiezhuanglü Si (the West Garden)

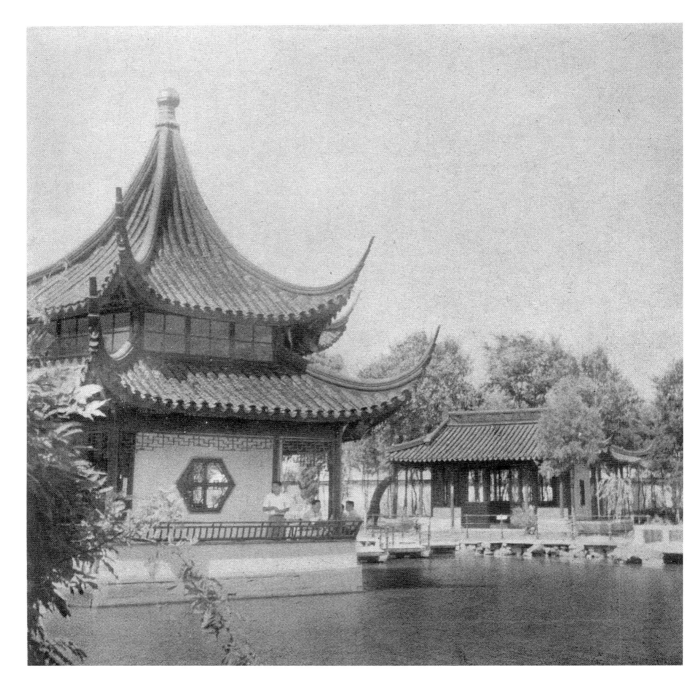

Winding rail steeps over
watery pearls;
Fresh breeze stirs up
emerald swirls.

曲檻俯清流
晴空搖翠浪

戒幢律寺西园湖心亭

Huxin Ting (the Mid-lake Pavilion) in Jiezhuanglü Si (the West
Garden)

The sun in the sky
strides; the shadow
in the corner hides.

景德路杨氏园

Yang's Garden on Jingde Road

Palms trees thrive by the
marble girded meadow;
Autumn air breathes into
curtained window.

芭蕉籠碧砌
秋聲先到簾櫳

沧浪亭
The Garden of Canglang Ting (the Canglang Pavilion)

花影疊重門

景德路杨氏园园门

Entrance Gate of Yang's Garden on Jingde Road

The green groomed bower reveling in late autumn glow.

一樓偓翠生秋暝

沧浪亭漏窗

Lattice window in the Garden of Canglang
Ting (the Canglang Pavilion)

修竹拂疏棂

沧浪亭漏窗

Lattice window in the Garden of Canglang Ting (the Canglang Pavilion)

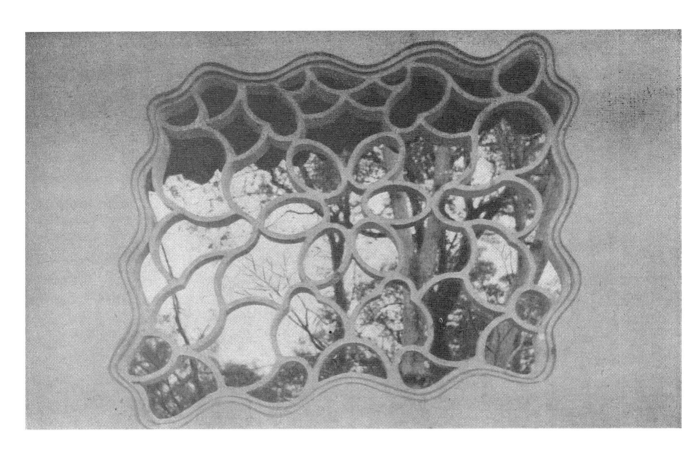

The phoenix tree
coveting the
sun-kissed window.

碧
梧
偷
戀
小
聰
明

沧浪亭漏窗

Lattice window in the Garden of Canglang
Ting (the Canglang Pavilion)

翠陰初轉午間花
深院聽啼鶯

沧浪亭御碑亭

Yubei Ting (the Imperial Stele Pavilion) in the Garden of
Canglang Ting (the Canglang Pavilion)

Winding pathway extends
far, far away; shadows of
osmanthus on the wall
sway; plum blossoms by
the window merrily play.

曲径通深窈
有墙头桂影
窗上梅花

沧浪亭步碕廊
Buqi Lang (the Buqi Corridor) in the Garden of Canglang
Ting (the Canglang Pavilion)

水閣無塵午晝長

沧浪亭复廊

The double-corridor in the Canglang Pavilion

Through ancient trees winds
a tranquil trail; emerald
luster shimmers all the
way to a blue hill; a grove is
dimly visible in the haze of a
dusk date.

古木通幽径
翠微踏路窄
晚烟丰隐平林

沧浪亭亭前

In front of the Canglang Pavilion

濃綠漲瑤窗
亂紅迷紫曲

仓米巷半园三曲桥

Sanqu Qiao (the Three Fold Zigzag Bridge) in Banyuan (Half
Garden) located in Cangmi Xiang

In the yard poplars are
everywhere found;
Around the garden apricot
trees abound;
On the wall moonlight
nudges shadows around.

綠楊庭院
青杏園林
月影又移牆影

畅园西面一角

West side of Changyuan (the Garden of Free Will)

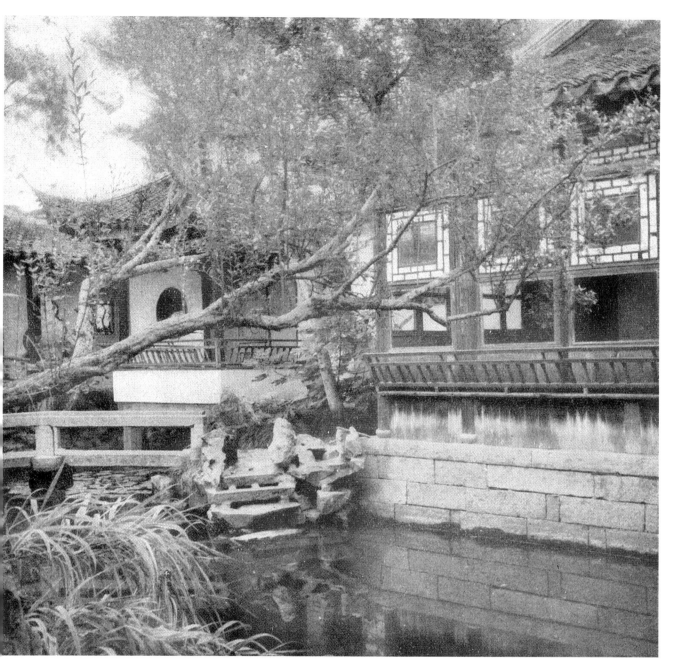

Let a branch it outgrow
the carved balustrade,
Alas, how much efforts
has vernal breeze made.

占斷彫闌八一枝
春風費盡纔工夫

畅园西面一角
West side of Changyuan (the Garden of Free Will)

The deep garden traps
vernal breeze;
The grey clouds hover over
the pond like green fleece;
The slim path is laced with
entangled trees.

深院鎖春風
正蔭綠池幽
交枝徑窄

畅园曲廊月门

Winding veranda and moon gate in Changyuan (the Garden of Free Will)

A pavilion stands quiet
on a crisp and starry
autumn night;
Along the corridor
crickets sing under the
frosty moonlight.

樓臺還清峭
冷蛩隨月到迴廊

畅园东面一角
East side of Changyuan (the Garden of Free Will)

Lain hushed and
flower scented trail.

芳径雨初晴

畅园小径铺地

Patterned pavement on a trail in Changyuan (the Garden of
Free Will)

水縱橫
石蓋龍

Crisscrossed waterways;
Dragonlike serpent
rockery.

附：无锡寄畅园石桥

Annex: A stone bridge in Jichang Yuan (Garden for Lodging
One's Expansive Feelings) in the city of Wuxi

Fed petals are washed quietly
down the rill.
Leaving the garden clearer
and greener still.

紅粉暗隨流水去
園林漸覺清陰密

附：无锡寄畅园

Annex: Jichang Yuan (Garden for Lodging One's Expansive
Feelings) in the city of Wuxi

幽懷倚石

附：无锡梅园

Annex: Meiyuan (Plum Garden) in the city of Wuxi

测绘图录编后附记
| Notes of the Survey Drawings

一九五六年五月，我率领同济大学建筑系建筑学专业二年级同学到苏州、无锡进行教学实习，主要对象是参观新旧及古典建筑，尤其对于苏州的园林我们又作为重点，在实习中进行了测绘。本集中的测绘图即该级同学的一部分成果。参加指导实习的除我兼总领队外，尚有我系教师王志英、朱保良、陈光贤三君，都尽了很多的力。特此一并附记。

陈从周

一九五六年十月

In May1956, I led the second year students with a major in architecture in Architecture Department of Tongji University to take a learning practice in the cities of Suzhou and Wuxi. Our main activities were visiting the traditional buildings in these two cities. In particular, we did an architectural survey on the gardens in Suzhou. The survey drawings collected in this book are a part of the result of this learning practice. Three other teachers, Wang Zhiying, Zhu Baoliang, and Chen Guangxian, have spent great effort in this practice.

Chen Congzhou

October, 1956

参加同学名单 | List of Students

沈在安 (Shen Zai'an)　陈世杰 (Chen Shijie)　殷焕圻 (Yin Huanqi)　张之俊 (Zhang Zhijun)　马光蓓 (Ma Guangbei)　杨维良 (Yang Weiliang)　沈鼎铭 (Shen Dingming)　朱有琳 (Zhu Youlin)　曹庆涵 (Cao Qinghan)　陈荣萱 (Chen Rongxuan)　焦璞文 (Jiao Puwen)　张纪延 (Zhang Jiyan)　黄宏骥 (Huang Hongji)　蒋守谦 (Jiang Shouqian)　叶佐豪 (Ye Zuohao)　陈峙 (Chen Qi)　程弋日 (Cheng Yiri)　刘纪芬 (Liu Jifen)　张景新 (Zhang Jingxin)　郑定国 (Zheng Dingguo)　王慧英 (Wang Huiying)　郁学儒 (Yu Xueru)　莫琴 (Mo Qin)　陈明 (Chen Ming)　郑国英 (Zheng Guoying)　赵群娇 (Zhao Qunjiao)　龙永龄 (Long Yongling)　郁操政 (Yu Caozheng)　高正秋 (Gao Zhengqiu)　沈瑞莲 (Shen Ruilian)　沈尧 (Shen Yao)　张华 (Zhang Hua)　李鑫林 (Li Xinlin)　赵凤珍 (Zhao Fengzhen)　王周云 (Wang Zhouyun)　唐班如 (Tang Banru)　林言官 (Lin Yanguan)　叶丹霞 (Ye Danxia)　陶祥兴 (Tao Xiangxing)　沈惠骥 (Shen Huiji)　胡圣儒 (Hu Shengru)　顾琪美 (Gu Qimei)　金福珍 (Jin Fuzhen)　钟临通 (Zhong Lintong)　谭华爵 (Tan Huajue)　施家谱 (Shi Jiapu)　殷鉴明 (Yin Jianming)　冯渭文 (Feng Weiwen)　朱培兰 (Zhu Peilan)　郑丽菊 (Zheng Liju)　苏邦俊 (Su Bangjun)　张聿洁 (Zhang Yujie)　安怀起 (An Huaiqi)　艾亨音 (Ai Hengyin)　戴天军 (Dai Tianjun)　朱谋隆 (Zhu Moulong)　曹书安 (Cao Shu'an)

在大家的鼎力相助下，中英双语的新版《苏州园林》终于问世了，距离中文初版《苏州园林》的诞生，岁月已逝去半个多世纪。"写得宏图欣得意，繁花开遍阖闾城"是父亲所作的《吴门杂咏》中的两句诗，表达了父亲对苏州寄予的厚望。我们希望新书的出版可弘扬中华的传统文化并告慰九泉之下的父亲。

父亲陈从周，是中国古典园林建筑学家，生前是同济大学建筑系教授，著有《说园》等许多园林著作，《说园》曾被译成英、日、德、法、意、俄等国文字，一版再版。然而，在这些书中，父亲最钟爱的还是《苏州园林》，把它称作是自己的"第一本书"。这本书不仅是父亲的成名作，更是他的所有著作中最不同寻常的一本书——它奠定了父亲的园林建筑人生以及在中国古典园林艺术界的地位，同时它也曾经给父亲带来苦难，使他饱受折磨。

这本书的内容最初是作为同济大学建筑系的教材使用，深受师生们的喜爱，一经出版，立即引起了社会的关注，并获得建筑史学界老前辈们的高度评价。据说，叶圣陶先生看到这

The new bilingual version (Chinese and English) of *Suzhou Gardens*, with the full back-up of all my friends, has come to light. It is over half a century since the publication of the original version of the book. "I paint the wonderland with pride and joy, to let flowers flourish all over Suzhou."

This is a poetic sentence from my father's *A Collection of Poems on Suzhou*, expressing his great expectation for the future of Suzhou. It is our hope that the new book will uphold the cultural heritage of China and bring consolation to our dear deceased father.

Mr. Chen Congzhou, my father, was a master architect of traditional gardens of China. He used to be a professor of the Architecture Department of Tongji University. He wrote numerous books and articles on gardens, including *On Chinese Gardens*, which has been published in English, Japanese, German, French, Italian, Russian and other foreign languages, and witnessed several printings or editions. But my father's favorite book is *Suzhou Gardens*, his first book, as he called it. This book is really a very unusual one. On one hand, it makes my father's name nationwide, establishing his position in the history of garden construction and the field of art of traditional Chinese gardens. On the other hand, it brought him many unexpected troubles and inflicted great suffering on him.

In fact, the original version of this book was only a course book used in the Architecture Department of Tongji University. Since its publication, it attracted widespread attention in the society. Senior doyens of architecture history had a high appraisal of the book. The teachers and students loved reading it. It is said that after Mr. Ye Shengtao (叶 圣 陶), the renowned scholar, had read this book, he wanted to see my father immediately. In Ye's mind, the person who is able to write such a wonderful book must be a senior scholar. To Ye's astonishment, he found when they finally met each other that my father was only a youth of over thirty years of age at the time of writing that book. Ever since, they became friends for dozens of years in spite of their age gap.

This book has deepened the awareness of China and the world of the gardens of Suzhou, though it was banished soon after its publication and then had a precarious fate. Through this book, the Metropolitan Museum of New York called on my father at the end of 1970s to design the Mingxuan (Ming Room, 明轩, or the Astor Court) in the Museum, based on Dianchun Yi (Late Spring Studio, 殿春簃) in Wangshi Yuan (the Master-of-Nets Garden, 网师园). From then on Suzhou gardens made their name in the world. At the same time, my father struck up friendship of nearly twenty years with Mr. I. M. Pei (贝聿铭), the world-famous architect. Mr. I. M. Pei said: "Mr. Chen Congzhou is a great master of his time in garden art. He is a benevolent gentleman and a good friend of mine. I got to know him in the 70s of the last century. I regret not having met him earlier." "Having such an intimate friend, I am immensely gratified."

In the mind of my father, Chinese garden construction is not an isolated architectural art. It is not only involved with the historical background of politics and economy, but also related with painting, poetry and drama. Mr. I. M. Pei speaks highly of my father: "Mr. Chen's understanding of Chinese garden art is thorough, profound and far above the pale of the average person."

My father studied painting under Zhang

本书后，便立即想结识父亲。在叶先生的想象中，陈从周应该是一位长者，不然怎么能写出这么一本书？但见面后，才知道父亲当年只不过三十多岁，之后，他俩便成了几十年的忘年交。

尽管命运多舛，出版不久就被打入冷宫，但这本书让中国乃至世界进一步认识了苏州园林。凭借这本书，二十世纪七十年代末，纽约大都会博物馆找到了父亲，于是便有了以网师园殿春簃为蓝本的明轩，苏州园林从此走向了世界，父亲和贝聿铭先生近二十年的友谊也从此建立。在为《陈从周传》所作的序中，贝先生写道："陈从周先生，中国园林艺术之一代宗师，仁人君子，吾之挚友。吾与从周初识于上世纪七十年代，恨相知晚也。每每聆听从周说园林、谈建筑、议评弹、论昆曲，甚为投机，畅须（聆）教益。得此知己，吾欣慰不已。"[1]

在父亲眼中，中国园林不是一门孤立的建筑艺术，它不仅有政治、经济的历史背景，还和绘画，诗词，戏曲息息相关。贝先生曾为之赞叹："从周对中国园林之理解肌擘理分，博大精深，非凡人能所及。"[2]

父亲曾师从张大千习画，起先习工笔，后来攻写意。二十世纪四十年代办过个人画展，出过画集，其中一幅《一丝柳一寸柔情》曾经蜚声沪上。画面上是一对羽毛初丰的小鸟，站在细细的柳枝上，卿卿我我。看父亲作画是一种美的享受，研墨、摊纸、润笔，稍停片刻，手臂在空中飞舞，笔尖在宣纸上疾行，转而狂舔着墨汁，继而又回到纸上跳跃。弯腰的兰、挺拔的竹、硕大的蕉叶，一一浮现在纸上。画上熟透了的葡萄快破皮了，他就赶忙把烟头移近，将漫开的水迹烘干。明代画家文征明曾为拙政园作画许多，父亲则是以山水画的视角赏园、品园，他认为："不知中国画理画论，难以言中国园林。"[3] 父亲造园、修园，用的也是绘画的手法，他强调"园以景胜，景以园异"，构园"有法而无式"[4]。他不拘泥于图纸，因地制宜，触景生情。"诗中有园，画中有园"[5]。天马行空的园林构思常常会使他随心而动地往纸上涂炭，往地上洒灰线（施工定位用）。这种设计方式虽然奇特，但父亲做来却是有章有序。

Daqian (Chang Dai-chien, 张大千). He learned Gonbi (a traditional Chinese painting method featured by fine brush work and detailed description) at first. And then he turned to the painting style of freehand brushwork. In the 1940s, he held his personal painting exhibition and had an album of paintings published. One of the paintings entitled "A Thread of Willow, A Length of Tenderness" once enjoyed high reputation in Shanghai. The painting features a pair of fledgling little birds perching on a thin willow branch and chirping sweetly to each other. To watch my father in the act of painting is indeed an enjoyment of beauty. He started by rubbing an ink stick against an inkstone, spread a large piece of Xuan paper and dipped his brush into the ink. After a little pause, he began to wield his arm in the air and let the tip of his brush sliding swiftly on the paper. Then he dipped his brush again into the ink and brought it back to continue its dancing on the paper. The bending orchid, the upright bamboo, the giant palm leaves all magically emerged on the paper. Finding that the ripe grapes on the painting seemed to burst, he hastened to bring a burning cigarette near them to dry up some overspreading ink water. Mr. Wen Zhengming, a famous painter of the Ming Dynasty, did numerous paintings for Zhuozheng Yuan (the Humble Administrator's Garden, 拙政园). In the same way, my father appraised and appreciated gardens from the angle of Chinese landscape painting. He held that "no comments on Chinese gardens are justified, without knowledge of the mechanism of Chinese painting." In the construction and reparation of gardens, he also resorted to the methodology of painting. He emphasized that "a garden excels in its landscape and landscape prides in being distinctive" and "there is no ready-made formula to follow in building a garden though there are some general guide lines to go by". In fact, he did not stick rigidly to the blueprint. And instead he often adapted his measures in light of local situations or made impulsive improvements at the sight of actual scenes. He advocated for gardens "embedded in both poetry and painting". He scrawled and splashed the sketch of a scene on paper and even sprinkled lime lines on the ground as dictated by flights of imagination. This way of designing seemed unusual but accorded with his own principles and procedures.

My father was keen on photography. The pictures he shot were full of import. The modern technique of photography gave full play to his profound understanding of Chinese painting. When I learnt picture-taking, my father taught me how to use small aperture and long exposure to display the details of things I shot. In order to turn out the charm of garden buildings, my father often put up the tripod and clicked the shutter. And then he sat down, lighting up a cigarette and quietly waiting for the end of exposure. In those years, my father used a German-made 120 film twin-lens reflex camera given him by my uncle Mr. Song Boqin when the latter left Chinese mainland. All the 196 pictures carried in the book *Suzhou Gardens* were produced by this camera. Mr. Ye Shengtao regarded these pictures as "all fine pieces of art and an pioneering undertaking in the fields of architecture and photography".

My father is diligent and well-grounded in literature, as he studied humanities at Zhijiang University under Mr. Xia Chengtao. Inspired by the sentiments of a man of letters, he inscribed his pictures with words ingeniously and painstakingly selected from Songci (poems of

父亲爱好摄影,照片拍得很有意境,他的绘画修养促使其把摄影技术发挥得淋漓尽致。我学拍照的时候,父亲就教我表现景物的细节要用小光圈、长曝光。为了在自然光下拍出园林建筑的神韵,父亲常常支起三脚架,按下快门,然后点上烟,坐在一边静静地等待曝光结束。当年父亲用的是一架德国双镜头120相机,是我四姨夫宋伯钦先生离开大陆前留下的。《苏州园林》书中一百九十六张照片都是用这架相机拍的。叶圣陶先生称这些照片"全都是艺术的精品:这可以说是建筑界和摄影界的一个创举"[6]。

父亲当年就读于之江大学文学系,曾师从夏承焘先生学词。父亲以文人的情怀为园林立意,别出心裁地撷取宋词为本书中的照片题款,煞费苦心。撷句的出处广泛,为了让词句更能传神,有些照片的上下句甚至撷自不同的宋词,有些词句父亲还改动了个别字以起到画龙点睛的作用。经过父亲再创作的文字与园林画面的完美结合可谓是出神入化,融合得天衣无缝。

父亲喜欢听昆曲，高兴时还会唱上几句，并善吹箫。夜深人静时，悠扬的箫音或唱词常伴随儿时的我和弟妹们进入甜蜜的梦乡。在父亲眼里，园林和昆曲同根而生，在他园林著作的字里行间也充满着戏曲元素。曲要静听，园宜静观，观之才有得，园景和曲景是不可分割的。中国园林中的一山一木、一榭一亭犹如舞台上一举一动、一词一曲，而园林韵律的曲折高下又与昆曲无二致；所以，父亲提倡要"以园解曲，以曲悟园"[7]。

就是这样，父亲的人文艺术修养在建筑领域里得到极大的发挥，他以画家的敏感、学者的严谨、考古工作者的刻苦精神，以现代建筑园林的眼光，以中国古典文学的风格著写了这本《苏州园林》。这是一部新形式的建筑史学专著。书中完整的园林建筑测绘图是当年父亲带领同济大学建筑系师生们手绘的。

《苏州园林》自一九五六年由同济大学教材科初版后，虽声名远扬，但发行量不多。一九八三年，这本书在东京以日文版的形式出版。适逢今日再版《苏州园林》，我们决心全书

the Song dynasty). His choice of poetic words came from wide-ranging sources and sometimes two consecutive sentences were quoted from two different Song poems in order to enhance their expressiveness. Occasionally he replaced one or two particular words to bring the poem and the picture to life. These recreated words matched the pictures of the book to a charm and attained the acme of perfection.

My father was found of Kunqu opera. When he was in a happy mood, he could even sing a few stanzas. He was a skillful player of Xiao (a vertical bamboo flute). In the day of yore, when the night was deep and quiet, the melodious music of the flute and the ballad often took my younger brother and sister and I into the sweet dreamland. In the eye of my father, gardens and Kunqu opera grew up from the same root. There were elements of drama running between the lines of his works on gardens. Music should be enjoyed when listened with bated breath; gardens should be appreciated when observed quietly and calmly for their best aesthetic effect. Melody and landscape are inseparable. It seemed to him that the hills, trees, pavilions and pagodas in a garden are just like the poses, movements, words and tunes of the stage art. In the same way, the undulating rhythm of gardens synchronizes with Kunqu opera. With this understanding in mind, he upheld all along the idea of "decoding music with the aid of gardens and reading the gardens by means of music".

In this way, my father's solid grounding and talents in art and literature were brought into full play in modern garden architecture. It was with the sensibility of a painter, the rigor of a scholar, the diligence of an archeologist, the vision of modern garden architecture and the style of Chinese classic literature that he brought the book *Suzhou Gardens* into the world. This is an update monograph on the history of architecture. The complete set of survey drawings of the gardens carried in the book are hand-made by the teachers and the students of the Architecture Department of Tongji University under the guidance of my father.

Since its publication by the Course-book Press of Tongji University, the book *Suzhou Gardens* became well-known far and wide, but its circulation was limited. Later in 1983, the Japanese version of the book was published in Tokyo. This time we decide to have the whole book translated into English, in the hope that the new version might help people nowadays to better understand and appreciate the brilliant garden culture of Suzhou.

The new version is the brainchild of the pains-taking efforts of two generations. My father's essays, like his paintings, are pithy, lucid and rich in meaning. The essays are characterized by an urbane and graceful narrative style and occasional passages, big or small, of lyric expressions. These essays also feature large loads of technical words of ancient architecture and of allusions to historical figures and documents. Due to the wide coverage of fields such as history, architecture, literature, painting and so on, to have the book translated into English adequately and vividly is by no means an easy matter. Mr. Chen Wei did the translation of the book *Traditional Suzhou Residences* a couple of years before, but to translate the essay "Analysis of Suzhou Gardens" in the present book is still a challenge. His English version has been revised and polished by Prof. Zhu Wenjun of Beijing Language and Culture University. The finalized English version comes up faithfully with

英译，希望世人能借此更好地欣赏与理解灿烂的中国古典园林文化。

新版本的完稿凝聚了两代人的艰苦努力。父亲的文章就像他的画，下笔简练，含意丰富，温雅婉约，娓娓道来。间或抒情，诗一般的文字，令人叹为观止。由于文中还有大量的古建筑专业词汇，并涉及许多历史人物与文献，所以要把这本涵盖了历史、建筑、文学、绘画诸领域的著作传神地译成英文，实在不容易。陈威虽然过去已经译过父亲的《苏州旧住宅》，对于这次的翻译工作仍颇感困难。本书译文经过北京语言大学朱文俊教授反复修改、润色后，精妙地表达了原文的含义。朱文俊教授曾在联合国教科文组织长期担任英译审校工作，去年再版的《说园》英译稿也是请他审校的。

更难能可贵的是这本书照片题款的英译。首先，为了寻找原书中这些宋词撷句的出处，张燾先生用现代网络搜索技术，搜索了近三万首宋词，为翻译奠定了基础，而其工作之艰辛足可以写成一部书。接下来的英文翻译就更具有挑战性了。朱文俊教授几易其稿，力图在义、音、形上都达到唯美的境界。我们相信，读者在阅读中会有所感受。新版《苏州园林》中每幅照片的宋词撷句由蒋启霆先生缮写，他曾为父亲的《说园》用小楷抄录了全文。

另外值得一提的是，本书的完成也称得上是一个群策群力的结果，得到不少专家和热心人的帮助，仅用"感谢"两个字难以表达我们由衷的感激。美国加州伯克利大学李林德教授翻译过昆曲《牡丹亭》，她多次来信指点我们从何着手；张熹不仅查找出宋词撷句的出处，还对书中的一些典故进行了考证；为了规范景点译名，苏州马汉鹏和曾澄夫妇几乎跑遍了苏州园林，找来了所有能找到的书中的景点译名，还实地拍了许多照片，提供了翔实的资料；苏州园林设计院有限公司贺凤春女士特地寄来苏州园林局撰写的《苏州古典园林》一书以供参考；徐正平费心地为我修改了这篇后记。

父亲去世已将近十年，我们为他做了几件事，包括筹建南北湖陈从周艺术馆，编辑《陈从周画集》，出版《苏州旧住宅》和《园综》，等等。从《苏州园林》初版到今天的新版，半个多

the original meanings, making the whole book a wonderful reading. Prof. Zhu worked for UNESCO for several years as a reviser. Last year he helped revise the English version of the second edition of my father's book *On Chinese Gardens*.

The English version of Songci attached to the pictures is worthy of particular mention. First of all, tremendous efforts were made to find out the sources of all those quoted Songci sentences. Mr. Zhang Xi availed himself of modern network technique for this challenging job. In the end he succeeded in ferreting out all the sources from among nearly 30 000 Songci, thus paving the way for the translation. Even more challenging part is the translation. Prof. Zhu revised his English version again and again in an attempt to perfect it as much as possible in meaning, sound and form. It is our hope that the readers may appreciate what has been done on our part and enjoy reading it. All the quoted Songci sentences in the current version were transcribed by late Mr. Jiang Qiting, who had done the transcription for the whole text of the book *On Chinese Gardens* in its year 1984 edition.

It is also worthwhile to mention that the publication of this book is the fruit of concerted efforts and generous assistance of some experts and helpful friends. To them we express our heartfelt and sincere appreciation. Prof. Lindy Li Mark of UC Berkely, who translated Kunqu opera *Peony Pavilion*, wrote to me several times about how to proceed with the work. Mr. Zhang Xi not only sought out all the sources of the quoted Songci sentences, but also made some textual research on a number of allusions in the book. Mr. Ma Hanpeng and his wife Mrs. Zeng Cheng visited almost all the gardens in Suzhou and collected all English names for scenic spots. They also took many photos on the spot to provide data and clues for later reference. Miss He Fengchun of the Limited Company of Suzhou Institute of Garden Designing sent by mail a book *Classic Gardens of Suzhou* written by the Garden Bureau of Suzhou. Mr. Xu Zhengping took pains revising the Afterwords part.

It has been almost a decade since my father passed away. In honor of his memory, we have done several things such as the preparation of the Nanbei Lake Art Gallery of Chen Congzhou, editing *Painting Album of Chen Congzhou*, having *Traditional Suzhou Residences* and *An Overview of Gardens* published, and so on. Over half a century has elapsed from the original to the present new version of *Suzhou Gardens*. During this period of time China has undergone profound changes. The thought of recalling the history and reviving the culture has inspired us to edit and translate the book *Suzhou Gardens*. Two years of persistent and painstaking efforts have drawn us to our father's side, to listen to his melodious flute and his enchanting stories about gardens. We feel so happy and so graceful to be nurtured again by his delicate sense of beauty. We are missing him so much. We will cherish the memory of our dear father forever.

Chen Shengwu

October, 2008

世纪过去了，中国发生了巨大变化。寻找历史、留住文化的想法激励着我们对《苏州园林》一书进行整理和翻译。历时两年的艰辛工作把我们重新拉到了父亲的身边——听园林，闻箫笛，又一次得到美的熏陶，受益匪浅。我们深深地怀念和感谢父亲！

陈胜吾

二〇〇八年十月

注：

1. 《陈从周传》，上海文化出版社 2009 年版。

2. 同上。

3. 陈从周《园林与山水画》，辑录于《陈从周散文》同济大学出版社 1999 年版。

4. 陈从周《中国的园林艺术和美学》，辑录于《陈从周散文》同济大学出版社 1999 年版。

5. 陈植为陈从周《春苔集》所作序，同济大学出版社 1985 年版。

6. 叶圣陶为陈从周《苏州园林》所作序，著于 1979 年 2 月 6 日，三联书店 1984 年版。

7. 陈从周《以园解曲，以曲悟园》，辑录于《陈从周散文》，同济大学出版社 1999 年版。

图书在版编目（CIP）数据

苏州园林：纪念版 = Suzhou Gardens（Centenary Edition）：
汉文、英文 / 陈从周著 . -- 上海：同济大学出版社，2018.11（2021.12重印）
ISBN 978-7-5608-8169-0

Ⅰ . ①苏… Ⅱ . ①陈… Ⅲ . ①古典园林—园林艺术—苏州—汉、英
Ⅳ . ① TU986.625.33

中国版本图书馆 CIP 数据核字 (2018) 第 218299 号

苏州园林
陈从周 著

英文翻译：朱文俊　陈威　　摄影：陈从周
封面摄影原作：陈健行（《苏州园林》，1994）
书名书法：陈从周　　题字书法：乐峰　　宋词撷句书法：蒋启霆

出　版　人　　华春荣
责任编辑　　武蔚　罗璇
责任校对　　张德胜
装帧设计　　博风建筑

出版发行　　同济大学出版社　　http://www.tongjipress.com.cn
　　　　　　地址：上海市四平路 1239 号　　邮编：200092　　电话：021-65985622
经　　销　　全国各地新华书店
印　　刷　　上海丽佳制版印刷有限公司
开　　本　　787mm×1092mm　1/16
印　　张　　23
字　　数　　574 000
版　　次　　2018 年 11 月第 1 版　　2021 年 12 月第 4 次印刷
书　　号　　ISBN 978-7-5608-8169-0
定　　价　　105.00 元